Going Back

GOING BACK

An Ex-Marine Returns to Vietnam

W.D. Ehrhart

McFarland & Company, Inc., Publishers
Jefferson, North Carolina, and London

Front Cover

Nguyen Thi Na, 67, Cu Chi District, Vietnam, December 8, 1985
(photo by W.D. Ehrhart)

Back Cover

Water buffalo, Cu Chi District, December 1985 (photo by W.D. Ehrhart);
photo of the author courtesy of staff photographer,
Commission of Investigation into War Crimes,
Socialist Republic of Vietnam

Library of Congress Cataloguing-in-Publication Data

Ehrhart, W.D. (William Daniel), 1948–
Going back.

Includes index.
1. Vietnam — Description and travel — 1975–
2. Ehrhart, W.D. (William Daniel), 1948–   — Journeys — Vietnam.
GFS AUTHORS,   I. Title.
DS556.39.E48   1987   915.97'0444   86-43085

ISBN 0-89950-278-4 (sewn softcover)
acid-free natural and enamel gloss papers

Printed in the United States of America

McFarland   Box 611   Jefferson NC 28640

For Anne
and for Leela

Acknowledgments

Sections of this book have previously appeared
in the *Philadelphia Inquirer Magazine, Indochina Newsletter*,
the Pendle Hill Pamphlet Series, and various editions
of the author's essay, "Learning the Hard Way."
Poems included in the text are reprinted
by permission from the following sources:
"Making the Children Behave," "Guerrilla War" and "Souvenirs,"
*To Those Who Have Gone Home Tired:
New & Selected Poems*, W.D. Ehrhart,
Thunder's Mouth Press, 1984.
"Country Scene," *Prison Diary*, Ho Chi Minh,
Red River Press, 1983.
"Mountains and Rivers of the Empire of the South,"
Ly Thuong Kiet, and "Questions Underground," Te Hanh,
Vietnamese Literature, Red River Press (no date).
"A Black Soldier Remembers," *Four Black Poets*,
Horace Coleman, BkMk Press, 1977.
"On Opening Le Ba Khon's Dictionary," *Blue Mountain*,
John Balaban, Unicorn Press, 1982.
"Sailing to Bien Hoa," *A Romance*, Bruce Weigl,
University of Pittsburgh Press, 1979.

Table of Contents

December 28, 1985

Nguyen Thi Na is 67 years old. She lives in a small hamlet in Cu Chi District, 35 kilometers west of the city that was once called Saigon. Her simple brick house was built for her only a few years ago by the People's Committee of Cu Chi, the Vietnamese equivalent of a county government. As I approach the house, half a dozen small children playing nearby stop and stare, then giggle nervously and scurry out of sight. Mr. Dao Van Duc, vice president of the People's Committee, takes my arm gently and gestures for me to enter the house.

Inside I bow uneasily to Mrs. Na and take a seat across the table from her. The walls are bare, except for a row of five identical certificates, each one framed in black and trimmed in red and yellow. I recognize the seal of the Socialist Republic of Vietnam on each certificate but cannot read the words, which are Vietnamese. Mr. Duc begins to introduce me, but before he has finished, Mrs. Na's eyes are brimming with tears.

"I gave all five of my sons to the revolution," she says through an interpreter, her toothless mouth trembling with the effort to maintain control of her voice, "and all five of them are dead." She gestures sharply to the five certificates hanging above her head. "I have suffered so much misery — and you did this to me."

She does not say: The Americans did this. She does not say: You Americans did this. "*You* did this to me," she says. It is uncanny, almost as if she can see me as I once was: a young American Marine slogging through flooded paddy fields, armed to the teeth, frightened and mean. The wrinkled, leathery skin of her face crinkles into a grimace, and the tears begin to fall onto the bare wood of the table between us. And I can only sit in stunned silence, dizzy from heat and shock.

Somewhere in the murky haze of my mind, words are moving — lines from a poem I wrote ten years ago called "Making the Children Behave":

1

Do they think of me now
in those strange Asian villages
where nothing ever seemed
quite human
but myself
and my few grim friends
moving through them
hunched
in lines?

When they tell stories to their children
of the evil
that awaits misbehavior,
is it me they conjure?

More than a decade later, I have my answer. I want to get up and walk out into the hot dusty afternoon and throw up in the road. I want to be home again in Philadelphia, in bed with my wife's arms wrapped warmly around me. Why have I put myself deeply into debt and traveled halfway around the world to confront such a terrible reality? What can I say to this lonely old woman who already knows what I am? This is not what I wanted, I think vaguely, as another wave of nausea washes over me; this is not it at all.

The Sands of Waikiki

What had I wanted? What had I expected? I'd known what I wanted back in February of 1967 when I'd gone to Vietnam that first time as an 18-year-old Marine volunteer. I'd grown up in the shadow of World War Two, that most noble of American crusades in which my father's generation had fought so proudly. As I child, I'd seen the newsreels of American soldiers liberating French villages: the soldiers dirty and smiling in their jeeps, the villagers weeping for joy and showering the soldiers with wine and flowers and kisses. I'd seen "To Hell and Back" a dozen times, and "Thirty Seconds Over Tokyo," and "Flat Top." I'd read *Guadalcanal Diary* and *Beach Red* and *The Battle of the Bulge*. I'd seen the fathers of my playmates each Memorial Day in Perkasie, the small town in which I'd grown up, marching in their American Legion uniforms, firing volleys of blanks from M-1 rifles while the solemn strain of taps wafted over Menlo Park from a single quavering trumpet. I knew the whole grand tradition of American heroism from Nathan Hale and John Paul Jones to Alvin York and Chesty Puller. I knew the Preamble of the Declaration of Independence by heart, and the Gettysburg Address, and Lincoln's second inaugural speech.

And I knew that courage and vigilance were still required. My schoolmates and I had practiced nuclear air raid drills in elementary school, huddling against the wall of the gymnasium, vaguely afraid, waiting for the missiles we knew the Russians could deliver because they'd beat us into space with the first artificial satellite. I'd seen Nikita Khrushchev on television, pounding his shoe on the podium of the United Nations General Assembly, shouting, "We will bury you!" I'd seen communism gain its first foothold in the western hemisphere barely 90 miles from the United States mainland. I'd lived through the frightening tension of the Cuban missile crisis, and had awakened one morning to the Berlin Wall.

3

So when Lyndon Johnson had stated unequivocally that if we did not fight the communists in Vietnam, we would have to fight them on the sands of Waikiki Beach, I had believed him. The United States was once again threatened. And now it was my turn to do my duty. And I had accepted that duty eagerly. I was going to be a hero. I was 17 years old, nine days out of high school, when I enlisted in the United States Marine Corps. Eight months later, willingly and without the shadow of a doubt about why I was there, I found myself in Vietnam. What I found in Vietnam, however, was not at all what I had expected to find.

I had been told that we were defending a free democracy. What I found was a military dictatorship rife with corruption and venality and repression. The premier of South Vietnam openly admired Adolf Hitler. Buddhist priests who petitioned for peace were jailed or shot down in the streets. Saigon officials at every level engaged in blatant black marketeering at astronomical profit and at the expense of their own people.

I had been told that South Vietnam (Republic of Vietnam) was waging a defensive war against communist invaders from North Vietnam (Democratic Republic of Vietnam), who were acting only as puppets for the Soviet Union and Red China. But during my first eight months in Vietnam, I found myself engaged in a small-unit war against guerrilla soldiers from the very villages and hamlets we were supposedly defending—soldiers who fought us with dud American artillery rounds rigged as mines, non-exploding punji stake boobytraps, and antiquated bolt-action rifles dating back as far as the French Indochina War. I did not actually engage North Vietnamese regular army soldiers until I had been in Vietnam for nearly a year.

I had been told that many Vietnamese civilians had been relocated to government-controlled safe hamlets to protect them from the Viet Cong. What I found was the wholesale forced removal of thousands of people from their ancestral homelands to poverty-stricken, misery-laden shantytowns where men had no work and women rooted through American garbage in search of food for their children.

I had been told that the Viet Cong managed to perpetuate their guerrilla war only through violence and coercion inflicted upon the Vietnamese people. What I witnessed and participated in was the random destruction of livestock, civilian homes and sometimes whole hamlets, the detention and often brutal interrogation of civilians, and the routine killing of unarmed men, women and children by the American military and its Saigon ally. The Viet Cong did not need to force people to support them or join their ranks; we were their best recruiters.

I had been told that the people of Vietnam wanted and needed our help, but I found that most people in Vietnam hated us because we destroyed their forests with chemical defoliants, and burned their fields with napalm, and called the people of Vietnam gooks, chinks, slopes and zipperheads, turning their sons into shoeshine boys and their daughters into whores. And most people in Vietnam, from what I could see, wanted little else than for us to stop killing them and go away.

I spent 13 months in Vietnam that first time, and for my small part in the war, my government promoted me to sergeant, awarded me the purple heart, two presidential unit citations, the Navy combat action ribbon, a division commander's commendation, the good conduct medal, and an honorable discharge. But in those 13 months, directly and indirectly, I had visited horror upon the people of Vietnam, and I could think of no good reason for any of it. And when I came home, it was not with pride, but with an overwhelming sense of shame, rage, guilt and confusion.

Eventually, after the United States invasion of Cambodia, and the killings of American students at Kent State and Jackson State, after the *Pentagon Papers* had proven beyond a doubt the years of deliberate lies and half-truths that had guided American policymakers and misguided the American people for a quarter of a century, after the Easter mining of Haiphong and the Christmas bombing of Hanoi, after the horror of Watergate had reduced the administration of Richard Nixon to richly deserved disgrace, I came to my own conclusions about Vietnam, and I was glad when the war finally ended in April 1975 — though by then it had all gone on far too long to allow for anything like rejoicing.

Since then, Vietnam has remained a permanent condition of my life — as much a state of mind as a geographical location, the turning point, the place where I first began to see and think and learn and question. I am not foolish enough to be unable to recognize that the cost of victory for "the other guys" was enormous and terrible. Seldom are there winners without losers, and during 30 years of constant war Vietnam was drained and devastated as few countries ever have been. I have often wondered what ever happened to Miss Chi, the beautiful young secretary who used to work at the National Police headquarters in Hieu Nhon. I have often wondered about Staff Sergeant Suong, the South Vietnamese army translator assigned to my battalion, one of the bravest and kindest men I've ever known. And what has happened to those once-familiar places I lived in and slept on and patrolled through and longed passionately to escape from forever? What have the Vietnamese done with their revolution? Are there any winners at all? What's it like back there?

For years I have wanted to go back. To walk along paddy dikes without fear of mines. To stroll through the streets of Hue that I had once helped to fill with rubble and bodies. To see green rice growing on that filthy lump of mud and barbed wire up along the Demilitarized Zone called Con Thien.

Catharsis? Curiosity? Adventure? Perhaps it is as simple as the Vietnamese proverb: "Go out one day; come back with a basket full of knowledge." Even as I worked to make the trip a reality, I wasn't really sure. And there in that small bare house in Cu Chi District, I was still not sure why I'd come. But I was absolutely sure that I had not come looking for Mrs. Na with her grief and her tears and her five framed certificates that had once been a family.

The Waiting Game

It is no easy task to travel to Vietnam. Ten years after the end of the war, the United States government still maintains an openly hostile posture toward the Hanoi regime — a kind of institutionalized sour grapes. There are no diplomatic relations between the two countries, and thus the Vietnamese have no visa-granting agency in this country because only an officially recognized embassy can grant visas. The Vietnamese Permanent Mission to the United Nations is enjoined by U.S. and international law from assisting American travelers in any way. Therefore, the only way an American can get a visa to travel to Vietnam is through a Vietnamese embassy in a third country. Theoretically, if you can get to one, any Vietnamese embassy will do — England, France, the Soviet Union, for example. But for practical purposes, the Vietnamese embassy in Bangkok, Thailand, is the one most accustomed to handling American travelers since Bangkok is the most common point of entry into Vietnam from the West.

But you can't simply fly halfway around the world and show up in Bangkok unannounced. To begin with, you've got to have an official sponsoring group in Vietnam such as the Foreign Ministry, the Cultural Ministry, or the Education Ministry, which requires making contacts. In addition, each request for a visa must be approved by the Hanoi government, which can take months and sometimes even years. Of course, they will not approve you unless they know something about who you are and what you want to do in Vietnam, and it is difficult to convey that information to them, since it has to be done indirectly through intermediaries.

If you can find your way through that maze, there is still the question of money. One can expect to pay $2,500–$3,000 in transportation, hotels, meals and other necessary expenses for a trip of less than a month's duration. Unless you are independently wealthy, or have a great job that pays well and allows you to take an extended leave without penalty—neither of which describes my condition—you've got to line up some kind of financial sponsorship. The entire process involved in arranging a trip to Vietnam can take years.

Four years, in my case. In late 1981, I was approached by a Canadian documentary filmmaker who wanted to take a group of Vietnam veterans back and make a film of the trip. Several United States television networks had expressed interest, and the Vietnamese were also interested. However, the Vietnamese would not grant visas or approve an itinerary until the filmmaker had a firm financial commitment, and the networks would not make a firm financial commitment until the Vietnamese cleared the visas and itinerary. The whole proposal hung fire for eight months before finally collapsing.

But the idea of going back had been firmly rooted in my imagination, and I put the word out among friends and acquaintances that I was looking for another opportunity. Nothing came of it for several years, but in 1984 I was approached by Greg Kane, then working for Vietnam Veterans of America, and Tom Bird, artistic director of the Veterans Ensemble Theatre Company, about joining a cultural delegation financed by VVA. The trip was set for July 1984. In the meantime, the Hanoi government had agreed to release the remains of several American MIAs, but only to a VVA delegation rather than directly to representatives of the United States government. The U.S. balked at the proposal, and the matter was still unresolved when the time for the trip came around. In that political climate, the Vietnamese decided that it would not be appropriate to receive a cultural delegation, and the trip was postponed until August. But by August, VVA's financial priorities had shifted and they were no longer willing to underwrite the trip.

I heard nothing further for more than a year. Then in late August 1985, Tom Bird called again to ask if I wanted to be part of yet another proposed cultural delegation. He had gotten funding from the Asian Cultural Council, and he would be able to tack a small group onto a delegation from the New York State Assembly that Kane, now working under his own organization called the Indochina Consulting Group, was organizing for mid-September. It was a difficult time for me to go; I had already made a number of professional commitments during the period the trip would be going. But I worked frantically for the next two weeks to rearrange my schedule so that I could go. Six days before the trip was to leave, however, there was a coup d'état in Thailand. Since the point of entry would be Bangkok, the New York delegation insisted on postponing the trip until the dust settled. Having rearranged my schedule once — at great inconvenience to myself and others — I could not go about doing so again. And that was the end of that trip.

Shortly thereafter, John Balaban called to ask me if I wanted to travel to Vietnam with him. John had been in Vietnam for several years in the late 1960s as a conscientious objector. He'd taught linguistics at the University of Can Tho until the university had been destroyed during the Tet Offensive of 1968. Then he'd become field representative for the Committee of Responsibility to Save War-Injured Children. Fluent in Vietnamese, he'd returned to Vietnam in the early 1970s where he'd spent 10 months wandering through the Mekong Delta, armed only with a tape recorder, collecting *ca dao*, traditional Vietnamese oral folk poetry. Since then, he'd become a professor of English and a very fine poet. I'd known him and his work for nearly a decade.

Sure, I'd like to go with him, I said. What's the deal? Back in early 1984, he explained, while traveling in Germany, a mutual friend of ours had met a Vietnamese general who'd invited him to visit Vietnam. The friend had asked John to accompany him, and together they'd set about the long and tedious task of seeking visas. Now in September 1985, the prospects for the trip were looking promising. The only catch was that our friend was no longer able to make the trip. Rather than letting the opportunity pass, John was trying to get the Vietnamese to approve the substitution of another friend of ours, Bruce Weigl — a Vietnam veteran who had served with the U.S. Army in the late 60s and who had also become an excellent poet and teacher in the years since. And as long as he was taking Bruce along, he'd thought, why not take me, too? Which sounded great to me.

But would the Vietnamese go for it? Only one way to find out, and we immediately began working on it through intermediaries in touch with the Vietnamese — primarily John McAuliff of the U.S.-Indochina Reconciliation Project. McAuliff had been to Vietnam half a dozen times already, had good contacts, and knew the ropes. There was nothing to do now but wait. In the meantime, however, I still needed to figure out how to pay for the trip. Once again, McAuliff came to the rescue: he knew someone who knew someone at the *Philadelphia Inquirer Magazine*, and by late November I'd struck a deal to write an article about the trip in return for what amounted to my airfare to and from Bangkok. That still left me with only half the money needed, but I had waited so long already — the strain of "going/not going" was taking a heavy toll — and my wife and I decided that we could afford the balance of the cost because this was important, if for no other reason than to get it over with.

Still, the prospect of the trip frightened both of us. Anne and I had only been married for five years, and except for a few brief occasions, we had never been separated, even overnight. In Vietnam, I would not even be able to call her; we would be separated for 22 days, and completely out of touch with each other during the 16 days I'd be in Vietnam. What if something should happen to one of us? It would be days before the other would even hear about it. Actually doing anything about it would be next to impossible. And now, with the trip almost a reality after all these years, it was suddenly possible to imagine almost every conceivable disaster. Anne found it difficult to sleep at night, and I found myself picking at her in that strange way we pick at those we love most. The tension between us mounted as the date of departure approached.

One part of me wanted to forget the whole damned thing and leave well enough alone, stay home with Anne and be safe and know that she is safe and not go digging around God-only-knows what old wounds and half-healed scars. But another part of me was drawn to this journey like a moth to a flame. The trip was scheduled to leave on December 12th. By December 7th, there was still no word on final visa approval.

Bangkok

Mr. Son, the consular officer at the Vietnamese embassy in Bangkok, has never heard of us. He turns the pages of a large register slowly, shaking his head back and forth, then turns toward us, shrugging almost imperceptibly, arms dangling at his sides, palms forward.

"I'm sorry," he says in careful English, "you are not listed here." He gives us a bemused look that could almost be taken for a smirk. "Many people want to go to Vietnam," he continues, "They come here and they do not understand. It takes time. If you want to fill out visa applications, perhaps in a few weeks. . . ." His voice trails off.

"But we have to be listed," John explains, "It's all been arranged." After waiting in suspense almost until the last minute, we had been told on December 8th—just four days before our departure from the United States—that everything was in order. McAuliff had confirmed it through his contacts. "Look here," says John, handing over a sheaf of letters and telex messages. All of them are documents that John has sent to the Vietnamese, however; because we could not be granted visas while still in the United States, there is no actual written confirmation from any Vietnamese official. All we have, finally, is McAuliff's assurance that our visas will be waiting for us in Bangkok.

But they aren't. Mr. Son leafs through John's papers, then gives John a look that suggests, "These don't mean jack-squat, fella," but says nothing. He puts them down on the counter between us. Bruce and I look at each other, shifting uncomfortably. Does this guy think I've come halfway around the world just for the hell of it? Just because I've got nothing better to do? I am trying hard not to let my anger become visible.

"There must be some mistake," I say, "We're writers. Poets." I hand him a copy of one of my poems that a Vietnamese friend has translated for me. He reads it and hands it back.

"You can fill out visa applications if you want to," he says, reaching under the counter and pulling out three cards. Again, there is that vague suggestion of a shrug.

"Look, there really must be some mistake here," John says. "Our sponsor is General Chi, vice president of the War Crimes Commission. This has all been arranged."

More silence. Then Mr. Son finally says, "Wait here, please." He disappears through a door at the back of the room. A dialogue of amazed obscenities transpires between the three of us. We flip through the pages of several English-language Vietnamese magazines lying on a table, light cigarettes, stare at the wall, look at each other and shake our heads. "There's no point in getting angry with this guy," John warns, "It won't help."

When Mr. Son returns, he asks us to fill out the visa applications. He explains nothing about where he's been or who he's talked to or what he's learned, but he seems noticeably less cool. As we fill out the applications, he tries to make small talk. "Whose war crimes are you investigating?" he asks with a laugh. At least he must have found out that we're not vagabond hippies passing through between Nepal and New Zealand, I think. Perhaps things will be okay after all.

"Call me tomorrow afternoon," Mr. Son explains as he collects the applications.

It is Saturday evening. We explain that our flight to Hanoi leaves Monday morning. Will we be able to pick up our visas tomorrow, we ask.

He gives us a long look and a bit of a wince. "Perhaps Wednesday, or Friday," he replies slowly.

"But our flight is Monday," says John.

"Please call tomorrow," Mr. Son replies, "That's all I can tell you. We will do what we can."

Back at the hotel, we try to confirm our Monday flight to Hanoi, but discover that the Air Laos office is closed until Monday morning. Then we call Korean Air Lines to confirm our return flight from Bangkok to New York on January 3rd only to discover that we are listed as stand-by only. Flights on the 5th and 7th are also booked full. We try to call the travel agent in New York who has arranged transportation, but he is gone for the weekend. Then we try to call McAuliff in Philadelphia, but he is out and we can only leave a message on his recording machine. There is nothing to do but wait, and hope.

Sleep is impossible. We've been gone a day and a half, and already

I'm exhausted, but I'm too keyed up to sleep. Nothing is working the way it's supposed to. In New York, we discovered that we were not booked "executive class" as we'd been told, but rather as regular coach passengers. In Anchorage, Bruce had his camera stolen from the men's room in the transit lounge. We'd been told we'd be able to use the VIP lounge during our four-hour layover in Seoul, but when we tried to enter, we were turned away at the door by several unsmiling men in dark blue business suits who looked like highly trained anti-terrorist security police; they had bulges under their suit coats that looked like pistols, and there was a clear suggestion that argument would be unhealthy. There was no telephone in the transit lounge in Taipei, so I was unable to call Anne as I'd promised. Then the taxi driver in Bangkok had pressed us hard to change our hotel accommodations before we'd even seen our hotel. "Much better hotel," he'd said, pulling out a photo album filled with beautiful young Thai women in various states of nudity. I'd thought of Anne half a world away, and I'd wanted to punch this jerk right in the mouth. And then we'd gone to the Vietnamese embassy. No, sir, things are not going well at all, I think as I try unsuccessfully to get some sleep.

On Sunday morning, there is still nothing to do but wait, so we decide to go sightseeing. We visit the Golden Buddha, then go to the Grand Palace — a truly fabulous complex of temples built over the years by the present ruling dynasty of Thailand — then walk through an outdoor market. The weather is balmy, and I'm wearing short sleeves and flip-flops only two days after leaving a dreary Philadelphia winter. This is Asia. It looks and feels and smells like Asia. I've never been to Thailand before, but I've been in Japan, Okinawa, Hong Kong, the Philippines, and of course, Vietnam. Here I am on the other side of the world for the first time in nearly 20 years, but it is impossible to enjoy it. All I can think of is our visas, and Anne.

After a harrowing ride back to the hotel in a three-wheeled Lambretta driven by a maniac who thinks he's Mario Andretti, we find a store and buy Buddhist prayer money and joss sticks. In front of the hotel is a small Buddhist shrine. We light the joss sticks and place them in the soil in front of the Buddha, then burn the prayer money. I want to pray for our visas, but something in me doesn't feel right about it. That isn't the kind of thing gods are much interested in, I think. Instead, I pray for Anne's safety, and for my safe return to her. We have performed this ritual twice already today, and each time I have prayed for the same thing, hoping that the visas will somehow manage to fend for themselves.

Once inside, nervous and apprehensive, we call Mr. Son. At last, there is good news: our visas have been approved, he says, and we can go in on schedule. He is very pleasant and apologetic. There was "a bureaucratic problem," he explains. General Chi is indeed expecting us, but his staff had not followed through with the Foreign Ministry and that is why we were not listed in the embassy's registry. We are to pick up our visas tomorrow morning on the way to the airport for the flight to Hanoi.

We are almost ready to celebrate, but there is still the problem of the "standby" flight for our return. If we take our scheduled flight to Hanoi, we will not be able to check with KAL before we go into Vietnam. Do we take a chance and go anyway? But McAuliff returns our call just as we are debating what to do. Don't worry about it, he assures us; he'll get us back to the States. Don't miss the flight to Hanoi. That night, we treat ourselves to dinner at a French restaurant up the street from the hotel. Later I call Anne; it will be 16 days before I will be able to call her again.

The next morning, we pick up our visas and go out to the airport. When we arrive, we check in with Air Laos to discover that only two seats are confirmed. One of us will have to wait on standby. But we *have* to go in together, we explain, you can't do this to us. We've got our tickets. Look at them. She is sorry, the woman explains, but there's nothing she can do. We'll just have to wait and see if the flight fills up or not. It is still two hours before departure. The next flight is not until Wednesday. As we wait, we quickly decide among ourselves that we'll all go in together or we'll all wait together, but we won't split up.

Vientiane

So it's really happening. After all these years, after all the false starts and dead ends and seemingly insurmountable obstacles, I am less than an hour's flight from Vietnam. Sitting in the transit lounge at Vientiane airport in Laos, in spite of the homesickness that gnaws at me like background static on a radio, in spite of the exhaustion of jet lag and lack of sleep and the strain of all the problems we've encountered since leaving New York, I can't help feeling giddily excited. What will it be like? How will I react? Soon I will finally know.

Somebody must have gotten bumped off the flight back in Bangkok. An hour before boarding, the Air Laos check-in clerk gave us three boarding passes and told us to go to the loading area. We hadn't asked any questions, though once we were aboard it was clear that the flight was full.

I'd flown on cruder aircraft during the war, but this was the most amazing commercial flight I've ever been on since the Air America C-47 I'd hopped from Dong Ha to Danang back in 1968 — and it might well be argued that no Air America flight could ever qualify as a commercial civilian flight since everyone knew, even then, that Air America was run by the United States Central Intelligence Agency.

In any case, the Air Laos twin-engine Russian-built turboprop that will take us to Hanoi via Vientiane is certainly a step down from what I've grown accustomed to. The seats are small, thinly padded and nonadjustable. Leg room is scarce. Overhead storage consists of open metal racks much like one finds on American commuter trains. The baggage hold has turned out to be the first three rows of seats: bags are simply stacked unsecured in-between, on and over the seats. I've been wondering nervously what would happen if the plane encounters any turbulence.

In-flight service is almost quaint. Before take-off, a stewardess came around with a tray of hard candies. Once in the air, we were served a cold meal consisting of a small sandwich made from French-style bread and some unidentifiable kind of lunch meat that looked somewhat like bologna, a small banana, a few cookies and several more pieces of hard candy, all washed down with weak tea served in glass glasses.

And now we are waiting for the plane to be refueled in Vientiane. The town is nowhere to be seen, but the airport seems little more than a sleepy county airstrip. Along the main taxiway, I can see a man lazily tending a water buffalo as it grazes on the foliage that grows right up to the edge of the tarmac.

Vientiane: capital of that most peaceful of countries that had slowly but inexorably been sliced, diced, chopped and slivered by the CIA and the legendary Vang Pao and his mercenary army, by the Pathet Lao and the north Vietnamese — a war that raged for decades largely beyond the prying eyes of the Western media and the American people. Am I sitting now where once had sat "Earthquake McGoon" and "Weird Neil" Hansen and "Shower Shoes" Wilson of Air America and the CIA, awaiting orders for yet another desperate flight to some beleaguered outpost on the Plain of Jars? Such picturesque and romantic names for such a dirty business. Had my friend John Clark Pratt, a former U.S. Air Force pilot who'd flown in Laos, once lounged here on this second-floor terrace, drinking beer and shaping the first thoughts that would one day become his remarkably revealing novel, *The Laotian Fragments?* Except for a few stripped-down rusting hulks of American aircraft off to one corner of the airfield, there is no evidence that the Americans have ever been here, no sign of the deadly little war waged in the shadow of Vietnam.

We order beer and are served three glasses poured from a large bottle with no label on it. Over at the "snack bar," someone is heating water: an aluminum pot sits on the back counter, and into it is thrust a bare electric coil plugged into a wall socket. We have been told to remain in the transit lounge separated from the rest of the terminal, but we discover that we can reach the main floor simply by walking out onto the balcony and into another door that deposits one at the head of the main stairs leading to the front entrance. There seems to be no apparent attempt to guard the door or the stairs or the front entrance. We could walk down the stairs and out into the Laotian afternoon and disappear, and no one would be the wiser. I have often been told that the Laotians are an easygoing people. "The sweetest people in the world," McAuliff has called them. Certainly, their airport is a laid-back affair.

On the balcony are two young men, perhaps in their mid-twenties.

They are wearing civilian clothes, and their hair is cropped short. They are speaking Russian, and are probably military advisors. I have never spoken to a Russian, except for expatriates. Who are these two men? What are they like? President Ronald Reagan has called their country "the evil empire," the source of all evil in the world. Are these two men evil? I find myself wanting to approach them and introduce myself. "I'm an American," I will say, "I used to be a soldier. I fought in Vietnam many years ago, and now I am going back in peace." What would it mean to them? What would they think? Would they care at all? The moment passes. I go inside and finish my beer.

And then we are airborne again, and when the plane lands this time, I'll be in Hanoi. Capital of the old Democratic Republic of Vietnam, and now capital of the unified Socialist Republic of Vietnam. The heart of the enemy, or so I had been told as an 18-year-old Marine. Symbol of defiance. Bruce tells the story of a former commander of his, back in the days of the war, who punctuated every order with the words, "On to Hanoi." Then he laughs. "I should send the guy a postcard," he says; "Hey, colonel, I finally made it."

And then we are crossing over the Red River, descending toward Hanoi, beginning our final approach. That day in late February 1968, when I climbed aboard that big silver "Freedom Bird" and flew away from Vietnam, still alive and all in one piece, I never thought I would ever see Vietnam again. Never in my wildest nightmares would I ever have imagined that I would want to. Strange, how the world goes around. Below us, I can see oxen and water buffalo, thatch-roofed houses, and dry ricefields separated by dikes. Scattered among the fields and houses are the pockmarks of craters left behind by American bombers fully 13 years earlier. Then the plane is on the runway. Off to our left are a row of Russian-built jet fighters parked in military revetments. The plane taxis to a halt, and we disembark and are directed to walk toward the terminal. Nearly 18 years have passed, and my world has come full circle.

Hanoi

Even before we're off the tarmac, we are met by a delegation from the Commission for Investigation into War Crimes. We're not hard to pick out, of course: there are few westerners aboard the plane, and as nearly as I can tell, we're the only Americans. Most passengers, both Vietnamese and foreigners, are directed to the customs lines, but we're taken right through and into a small waiting room where we're served coffee and offered Vietnamese cigarettes while introductions are made. It pays to have influential friends, I think to myself, thankful that I don't have to unpack my luggage.

Our interpreter is Duong Van Loan, a young woman of 25. The oldest member of the group is Nguyen Hoang, introduced as the "chief of bureau," who looks to be 65 or 70, but it becomes apparent quickly that the person in charge is Ngo Thi Troan, a woman of about 45 or 50. Her official title is "chief of foreign relationship section." Also present are two men about our age, perhaps a few years younger, who are drivers. General Tran Kinh Chi, vice president of the commission, will receive us later that evening, we are told.

The awkwardness of meeting new people in a strange setting is compounded by the language barrier. Miss Loan will prove to be a personable and thoughtful guide over the next week, but she is just out of language school, on her first assignment, and her vocabulary is limited, her pronunciation weak. We had counted on John's being able to do much of the translating, since he had once been nearly fluent in Vietnamese, but we discover that he's gotten more than a little rusty in the past 14 years; he has lost much of his vocabulary, and though his pronunciation is still good, the northern dialect is very different from what he'd learned in the south. Everyone smiles a lot, drinking coffee and chain-smoking cigarettes with studied determination.

I am wondering what we're waiting for when a uniformed customs officer appears at the door and motions to Mrs. Troan. There is a brief conversation in Vietnamese between the officer, Mrs. Troan and Miss Loan, then Miss Loan explains that she is sorry but we must go through customs after all. So much for influence, I think. I have nothing to hide, but I've managed to pack everything for the trip into two small bags, and I dread the thought of having to tear it all apart just to prove that I'm not a cocaine smuggler.

And indeed, everything is torn apart, slowly and methodically. First, we must fill out declaration forms. Then we must account for all of the currency we're carrying, and the amount we physically show the officer must match what we've written on the forms. Bruce is off by $5, and the officer sternly points this out as he ceremoniously corrects the figure written on Bruce's form. Then, John's and my cameras are inspected. Finally, one at a time, each of us must empty our bags for the officer. When my turn comes, I decide to explain carefully and deliberately each and every item I am carrying. If these guys have nothing better to do, so be it.

These are books, I begin. The officer starts to shove them aside, but I quickly pick one up and open it. See, it's poetry, I tell him; I wrote it myself. I'm a poet. I reach into my pocket and hand him a copy of the one poem I have in translation. You can have it, I tell him; take it home with you; show it to your friends. These are cans of tobacco, I tell him. I show him the loose papers, explaining that I roll my own: it's cheaper, I say, I don't smoke so much, and it's better tobacco. Take a whiff, I add, opening one of the cans and putting it under his nose. He pushes the cans aside. Toothpaste, I continue, holding up a tube, unscrewing the top and squeezing out a small dollop. I rub it on my teeth and smile. Long sleeve shirt. Short sleeve shirt. Shaving cream. On through the first bag and into the second one. Finally, less than halfway through my second bag, the young officer impatiently waves his hand at me, indicating that the inspection is over. But there's more, I indicate with a gesture. I repack my bags and follow the others out of the terminal, smugly celebrating my small victory.

Outside, the city is nowhere to be seen. John, Bruce and I pile into the back seat of a small Japanese car while Miss Loan gets in front with the driver. Mrs. Troan, Mr. Hoang and the other driver follow us in an enclosed military-style jeep. It is late afternoon, and people are clearly headed home after a day of work; the roads are clogged with pedestrians, ox-carts and bicycles. I am trying to take in everything I see: the crowded, poorly-paved road, the people, bare fields, brick-making kilns, political

posters and banners—but fatigue and reverie and the bumpy ride and
the constant blaring of the horn make it hard to concentrate. It is rapidly
becoming dusk, but our driver turns on his lights only on those rare occasions when another vehicle is approaching. Headlights must be scarce:
other cars and trucks seem to be doing the same thing, and of the few
vehicles we do encounter, many have only one headlight.

It is hard to judge how far we have traveled because the odometer
doesn't work, but it's a good half-hour or more before we reach the edge
of the city. And when we do, we do so abruptly. A city of perhaps two
and a half million people, Hanoi doesn't have suburbs the way American
cities do. One moment, you are in the countryside; the next moment you
are in the city—or so it seems. Then the steady stream of bicycles abruptly
becomes a deluge, and the driving—already mildly harrowing—takes on
the attributes of a game of vehicular pinball. There are no streetlights,
and few of the bicycles have lights or even reflectors.

In a country where spare parts are scarce and fuel is at a premium,
bikes have long since become the workhorses of everyday life. I have read
about this, but it is still awesome to witness. There are bicycles bearing
loads of cordwood stacked eight feet high. Bikes with large earthenware
jars strapped to either side of the rear wheel. Pedicabs, called cyclos.
Tricycle trucks, both motorized and pedal-powered. Bikes loaded with
baskets of potatoes or coal. Bikes with one, two and three people aboard.
Twenty years ago, when the Ho Chi Minh trail was nothing but a series
of rough tracks in the jungle, the Vietnamese army used bicycles to haul
everything from ammunition to medical supplies 1,000 miles through a
rain of American bombs to the battlefields of the south. So this is how
they did it, I think, as the impossible stampede of bicycles swarms all
around me.

Trucks and cars are scarce. Most motor vehicles in Vietnam, we will
soon learn, are old, repaired and jury-rigged many times over, and
stripped of almost every accessory. Except the horn, that is: it is not possible to navigate around and through the press of bicycles without the horn.
One starts the engine and the horn simultaneously, and the horn is never
silent until the engine stops running. Still, cars, trucks, ox-carts and bicycles seem remarkably considerate of each other. To look at the apparent
confusion on the roads and streets, it is impossible to imagine how the
Vietnamese avoid strewing bodies all over the place. Two dozen times on
the road from the airport to the hotel, my heart has been wedged between my teeth, just waiting for the sickening thud of metal striking
flesh. But it hasn't happened even once. Nor will it in the 16 days to come.

When we reach the hotel, we are told that General Chi will receive us in one hour. Mrs. Troan points to a three-story U-shaped building directly across the street, and Miss Loan explains that the offices of the War Crimes Commission are inside, along with the Ministry of Labor and the Ministry for Social Welfare and Invalid Veterans. Our hotel is the Thong Nhat, meaning Unification. In the time of the French, it was called the Metropole. It appears to have seen better days, but there isn't time to look around. There is hardly enough time to check in, find our rooms and get cleaned up before we must leave for our meeting with the general. I don't want to meet the general tonight. I don't want to meet anyone. I am bone-weary. I feel dizzy. I want to sleep.

It is "winter" in the north; though it's not raining, the sky has been overcast since we arrived and the temperature this evening is in the mid-40s. I pull on a sweater and go down to the lobby to meet Miss Loan, John and Bruce. Outside, the street is dark and there is little traffic of any kind. The courtyard of the ministry building is dark. All the lights in the building are off except for a few lights visible on the third floor. We pick our way carefully up the staircase and walk down a hall toward the lights. The building, like the hotel and most other major buildings in Hanoi, is of French design; it looks vaguely Mediterranean. The hallway runs along an external wall, and there are no windows facing the courtyard, but only louvered shutters drawn open to admit the chilly night air and what little light the night has to offer.

General Tran Kinh Chi is waiting at the door of a large conference room to greet us. He is a short man with gray hair and thick glasses, but his handshake is rock-hard and unflinching. He is wearing dark trousers and a heavy pullover sweater. Inside the room is a large table covered with white cloth and surrounded by perhaps a dozen chairs. Those who met us at the airport are waiting for us, along with several other men. One of them is a Mr. Quang, an interpreter on loan from the Foreign Ministry. I never really figure out who the others are. Mr. Quang's English is extremely good.

The table is spread as if for a party. There are bowls of tangerines and bananas and a small green fruit I soon discover to be Vietnamese apples, dishes of candied nuts called "wedding fruit" that look as though they might be garbanzo beans, a pile of what looks to be small gifts wrapped in fibrous green leaves, and numerous packs of Vietnamese cigarettes. A young woman pours coffee as the general picks up a pack of cigarettes and offers them to us. The cigarettes, in a green and white wrapper, are called Dien Bien, commemorating the great Vietnamese victory over the French in 1954. On the front of the pack is a reproduction of Viet Minh soldiers raising, Iwo Jima–style, the starred flag of the Democratic Republic atop the last French bunker to surrender. The general lights our cigarettes, then lights one for himself. He dishes two heaping spoonsful of coarse brown sugar into his coffee, then pushes the sugar bowl toward me.

"What would you like to do while you are here?" he asks through Mr. Quang. I explain that I would very much like to see Hue, and perhaps Danang and Con Thien, Hoi An, Quang Tri—the places I had been as a soldier. Bruce wants to go to central Vietnam also. John says he would like to go to Can Tho and Con Phung Island in the southern Mekong Delta. We would all like the opportunity to meet with some Vietnamese poets and writers. Beyond that, we say, we haven't anything special in mind. We're poets, we explain, observers. We have come to see and learn. To feel and smell and taste and experience—whatever the general thinks would be good for us to do. What does the general think we should do, we ask.

"Eat," the general says with a clipped laugh and a gesture of the hand, "It's no good to talk on an empty stomach." The coffee cups have been removed, and the young woman has poured tea for everyone. There are no seconds on coffee, but the teacups will be kept full all evening. General Chi reaches across the table and offers me a banana. I'm not hungry. I'm tired. And I'm worried by the evasiveness of the general's response to our requests. But the general clearly wants me to have this banana, so I take the banana and begin to peel it.

As I'm doing this, the general puts one of the leaf-wrapped bundles on each of our plates. Grateful for the excuse to put aside the banana, I unwrap the package to discover a sweet, green, sticky pastry with a con-sistency somewhere between pound cake and stiff jello. It is quite good, actually, and I find myself wishing I had the appetite to enjoy it fully. I eat half of it, then begin to roll one of my own cigarettes, but the general immediately offers me another Dien Bien. It is no use trying to explain that I don't like packaged cigarettes, Vietnamese or American. I take the Dien Bien and he lights it for me.

Finally, General Chi sits up straight and pushes his plate aside, Mr. Quang takes out a pen and tablet, and we are ready to get on with business. But the first thing the general says is that we can't go to Hue or anywhere else in central Vietnam. Why not, I ask much too quickly and sharply. There has been a typhoon, he explains, the worst in forty years, and the damage has been extensive: bridges destroyed, trees uprooted, homes flooded and collapsed, roads washed out. Many people have been killed and many more have been left homeless. Travel is difficult, even for those who live there; for us, it is impossible to arrange. He is very sorry.

I can't believe what I'm hearing. I've left my wife alone during the Christmas holidays, put myself $1500 into debt and traveled halfway around the world—and I won't even get so much as a glimpse of the places in which I'd fought?! What in the hell is going on here? What's gone wrong? I've been telling our contacts ever since September that it is absolutely essential for me to get to Hue. The editor at the *Philadelphia Inquirer* is expecting an article based on my visiting at least some of the places I had been before. I *want* to see those places. I *need* to see them. I can't believe it. I can barely keep my composure as the general explains to John that Can Tho is probably not possible either because of the time it would take away from the agenda that has already been planned.

Planned agenda, I think angrily to myself. So now the truth comes out. Why didn't you tell us that in the first place? Why the hell did you bother to ask us what *we* wanted to do?! As I sit in stony silence, still fighting to keep my composure, the general proceeds to outline a lengthy and detailed agenda that largely revolves around various aspects of the work of the commission. I am too distraught even to bother writing it down, but it mostly seems designed to teach us about the crimes of the United States government against the Vietnamese people. Just what I need, I think bitterly, a propaganda rap. Christ, I've spent 18 years studying the war. I know all about who did what to whom. You don't *need* to convince me. Show me what you've done with this country *since* the war; that's what I came here to see. The remainder of the audience passes in a blur.

Back at the hotel, John and Bruce are startled by the depth and force of my anger. "I didn't come here to be preached at," I tell them, "What kind of idiots do they take us for?" John urges me to be patient, to let things ride for a few days and see what develops. Bruce points out how selfish it is to want to go to central Vietnam when so many people are suffering such hardships there. I don't care. I'm tired, and I can't think. I want to leave immediately, but John reminds me that even if I were to do so, it would probably take days to arrange.

Later, alone in my room, I am still too wired to sleep. Hanoi. And Saigon—renamed Ho Chi Minh City in the first flush of revolutionary fervor. That's all I get to see? Who the hell cares about Hanoi and Ho Chi Minh City? My friends died in places called Ai Tu and Phuoc Trac.

I need to see those places again, to see children playing and old men tending water buffalo on the once-bloody soil upon which I'd nearly died. I have dreamed of those places for years. Not a day of my life has passed in nearly two decades without thinking of them. I am only now beginning to understand just how far I have come, physically and emotionally, to see them, even for a few hours: to close the circle; to make the world truly come around. And it has all been for nothing.

I stretch out on the bed only to discover that a permanent sag in the mattress hurls me involuntarily into a tight fetal ball. I suddenly become acutely aware of the shabbiness that surrounds me. The single naked lightbulb dangling from the ceiling. The cracked plaster on the walls. The missing tiles in the bathroom. The missing knob on the closet. The cracked mirror. The light switch on the wall that looks like it's just waiting to electrocute me. Even the communal toilet in the room down the hall won't flush.

I do not want to be here. What will I do for the next two weeks? I have been telling myself for months that I'm not expecting anything, that I'm wide open to whatever may happen. Now I have to realize that I've arrived with all sorts of expectations and extra baggage. It's embarrassing, mortifying. I have been lying to myself for months — for years. It is hard for a man of 37 to have to come to terms with his own foolish romanticism.

Tuesday, December 17

I am lying in a steep valley surrounded by a strange mist. For a moment, I am not quite sure where I am. Then, as I begin to wake up more fully, I remember that I am alone in my room at the Unification Hotel in Hanoi. The illusion of sleeping in a valley is created by the unyielding sag in the bed; the mist is actually the mosquito net, which covers the bed like a four-poster canopy. I am immediately depressed. I want Anne, but she's on the other side of the world. I can't even call her. What if something should happen — who knows what? What if I should never see her again?

I get up with a headache and walk down the hall to the toilet. The hall is not heated, and the air holds a chilly edge. The toilet still won't flush, but someone has cleaned it out during the night. I return to my own bathroom, which contains a sink and a bathtub. I brush my teeth using boiled water from a bottle on the glass mantel over the sink — at least I hope it's boiled; I have been warned by McAuliff to drink only boiled water, not water straight from the tap. The bathtub is fitted with a showerhead attached to a flexible rubber hose, and I squat down in the tub and give myself a kind of shower, holding the showerhead in my hand. I am surprised and grateful to discover that the hot water works. I dry myself on a small pink hotel towel no larger than a dish-towel.

The menu in the hotel restaurant is written in French, so John has to translate for me. Most of the entrees are western style dishes such as omelettes, and the selection is limited; the whole menu, a typed carbon-copy, fits on a single small sheet of lightweight paper. I order coffee, papaya and *pho*, a traditional Vietnamese dish rather like noodle soup which the Vietnamese seem to eat for breakfast, lunch or dinner. A few of the other tables are occupied — almost entirely by foreigners: Germans, Japanese, an English-speaking couple with two small children —

but most are empty. A half-dozen or so waiters and waitresses stand around toward the side of the room closest to the kitchen, as if waiting for something to do. We receive two bills, one for food and one for beverages, which are calculated in dong—the currency of Vietnam.

By the time we are finished, Miss Loan is waiting for us in the lobby. She is wearing tight-fitting blue jeans and a heavy coat. The streets are again awash in bicycles, along with a few cars and trucks, and now and then an oxcart with heavy rubber truck tires driven by a small boy who stands on the cart brandishing a thin flexible stick like a charioteer. A few of the cars parked in front of the hotel carry diplomatic license plates. Walking, we cross a small beautifully flowered park dedicated to Indira Gandhi, then pass beneath the gaze of an immense portrait of Ho Chi Minh perched atop the Central Bank Building. We enter a smaller bank several blocks further on where we can change U.S. dollars into dong.

First we must fill out currency exchange forms in triplicate. There is no carbon paper, so each copy must be filled in separately. The teller gathers up our forms and disappears. Fifteen minutes later, she returns and motions us to a separate counter. But when she sees that we have traveler's checks, she begins to speak rapidly in Vietnamese to Loan. Without waiting for Loan to reply, she tears up the old forms and gives us different ones, each to be filled out in triplicate, one at a time. Then she disappears again. While we are waiting, we notice that other tellers are giving away 1986 calendars. When we ask if we, too, can have calendars, we are told that they are only for customers with accounts. Some things seem to be the same the world over.

When our teller returns, she hands John a stack of dong for his traveler's checks. Then she does the same for Bruce. But when I hand her $150 in traveler's checks and a $50 bill, she suddenly looks as though she's swallowed a goldfish. There is another little powwow between the teller and Loan, then Loan asks me if I have any other traveler's checks. Back at the hotel, I tell her. She translates for the teller, who replies in Vietnamese. Do Bruce or John have any other checks with them, Loan asks. John writes out a check for $50 and gives it to the teller, I give John the $50 bill, and the teller gives me 2,813 dong—a shade over 14 to the dollar. Is everything this difficult, I ask Loan as we leave. It has taken nearly an hour to complete the transaction. Loan just giggles.

Back at the hotel, Mrs. Troan, Mr. Hoang and our two drivers are waiting. We pile into our two vehicles and take off across town, being informed along the way that we must register with the local police headquarters. When we arrive, we are greeted at the door by a middle-aged colonel of police who ushers us into a small receiving room. We are served tea, tangerines and cigarettes while we fill out forms similar to our customs declarations, again in triplicate and without carbon paper. The colonel asks for our passports and visas, then asks for additional photographs. We don't have any more, we explain; no one told us we would need them. He gives us a mildly impatient look, says something to Mrs. Troan, then gestures as if to say, "no matter." He thanks us and rises, indicating that the meeting is over. What about our passports, I ask Loan. There is a conversation between Loan, Mr. Hoang and the colonel, then Loan says that we'll get them back tomorrow. I am more than a little uneasy about surrendering my passport, but there is nothing to be done about it.

Back at the hotel, we are told to be at the commission's offices in the ministry building at 1 p.m., and when we arrive, the same group that was present the previous night is waiting for us. The fancier foods are gone, but there are bowls of tangerines and bananas, and we are served coffee immediately, followed by tea. I give General Chi a copy of the one poem I have which has been translated into Vietnamese. He folds it up and puts it in his pocket. He has a stack of typed notes on thin yellow paper in front of him. He asks if we have any questions before we begin.

Tell us about yourself, Bruce asks. That's not important, he replies through Mr. Quang, who is again translating for the general. But Bruce presses him, explaining that people back home will want to know who is this man who has been our sponsor and host. With apparent reluctance, he begins by saying that he is 57 years old and has seven children. All of them have served in the army at one time or another, and one son is still a colonel on active duty. General Chi became a political cadre in 1943 at age 16, even before the army was founded, then joined Ho Chi Minh's Viet Minh as a soldier in 1945. His father, who was a teacher, was also a guerrilla fighter. He has lived through three wars, he tells us: the August Revolution of 1945, when Ho declared an independent Democratic Republic of Vietnam, the French war of 1946–1954, and the war with the United States.

Where did you meet your wife, we ask. In the army, he replies; everyone was in the army then. "When the enemy comes to your house," he says, "everyone fights." Did you ever fight against Americans, we ask. No, not directly; he was stationed mostly in the north, though occasionally he would travel south, mostly to Tay Ninh Province and the Central Highlands. Though he is good-natured and often humorous, each answer is short and without embellishment. Is he just naturally modest, I wonder, or is it a political sin in the collective state to speak too much of self? I have no way of knowing.

Finally, he indicates that he's said enough about himself. He finishes by pointing out emphatically that he is no longer an active general. "When the nation is at war," he says, "we are soldiers; when there is peace, we go on to other things." Now he is vice president of the war crimes commission, which we find out later is the equivalent of a vice minister. He shuffles his papers as though anxious to begin.

Who were the best soldiers, Bruce asks. The general throws back his head and laughs heartily. He makes a sound like a good-natured growl, and I wonder if he's weighing the potential for embarrassment that an honest answer might yield. "If the Americans were the best soldiers," he replies finally, "we could not defeat them." He goes on to explain that individually, the Americans were physically stronger and had better weapons and supplies. Many fought strongly and bravely. In a just war, the United States military could not be defeated, he says, citing World War Two as an example, but an unjust war automatically leads to defeat; the United States lost because the war was unjust. He tells a story about an American colonel, shot down over the north, who asked to meet the pilot who had downed him. The colonel, 50 years old, was surprised to see that his adversary was so young. How could such an inexperienced pilot have defeated him? "I was more determined than you," the general recounts the young pilot's reply.

Victory does not belong to force of material, he explains, but depends "on the way of fighting. A swarm of bees is sometimes better than an elephant." Mobile foot soldiers are better than noisy helicopters. Boobytraps made from dud bombs are better than the bombs themselves. Special units of five or six soldiers can disable an entire airfield. American soldiers could not fight the way Vietnamese soldiers could fight, he says, because they lacked surprise, they lacked the support of the people, and they lacked force of will. The Vietnamese people possessed the "heroic spirit" of the independence struggle. American soldiers were misled; they were told they were fighting communism, but they could not understand who they fought, or how, or what for.

This "heroic spirit," the general explains, predates Marxism-Leninism. It is inherent in the will of the people, and Vietnamese history demonstrates this time and again. Still, the long struggle for independence could not have been won without Marxism-Leninism. Marxism-Leninism teaches the Vietnamese to distinguish between the progressive American people and the reactionary United States government. It allows the Vietnamese to determine the strengths and weaknesses of the United States government. It provides the "correct line" in fighting—knowing how to fight against the enemy and how to overcome difficulties. "When we have the right line," he says, "we are supported by the progressive peoples of the world, including the American people."

It is a refrain I will hear often in the next two weeks, this concept of the progressive American people. I think of the general indifference of most Americans toward Vietnam today, of the strident hostility of such groups as the various POW/MIA organizations, the VFW and the American Legion, Ronald Reagan's assessment of Vietnam as "a noble cause" and his two lopsided election victories, the overwhelming popular support for the invasion of Grenada. Does General Chi understand that the "progressive American people" may well be a group far smaller than his words would suggest, I wonder; does he really believe that most Americans stand in opposition to their government?

Other phrases draw my attention. General Chi invariably speaks of the American people and the American government as two distinct entities, but he never refers to the government of Vietnam; it is always simply "the Vietnamese people," as if government and people are synonymous. I am skeptical, but I find myself remembering the words of various presidents of my country over the years: "The American people will not tolerate a communist invasion of South Vietnam"; "the American people oppose communist insurrection in Central America"; "We must support the Nicaraguan people in their struggle to throw off the oppressive yoke of the Sandinistas." Is General Chi's language anything more than a mirror image of what I've heard in my own country all my life?

Nor does the general ever refer to the old government of south Vietnam as anything other than "the puppet regime." Similarly, the old army of the south—the Army of the Republic of Vietnam, or ARVN, as we called them—is invariably referred to as "the puppet army" or "the puppet troops." It sounds like stock political rhetoric, which it undoubtedly is—but though our South Vietnamese allies regularly proved to be less malleable than most American policymakers would have wished, historically there is more than a little truth to the general's phraseology. And indeed, to those who fought on the general's side—and not without reason—the Saigon regime was surely never for a moment possessed of so much as an ounce of legitimacy.

What was the most difficult time during the war, I ask. 1965, he replies, when American combat troops arrived and planes began to bomb the north systematically. It was then that the Vietnamese came to understand that China would betray them, that the Chinese did not support the Vietnamese struggle. Before 1965, China sent soldiers and antiaircraft batteries to help defend against U.S. planes. But in 1965, the Chinese refused to match the U.S. build-up. It was a clear signal, says the general, that as long as the United States did not attack China, China would allow the United States to do whatever it wanted to Vietnam. Also, until 1965, Soviet and Eastern European supplies of food, fuel, weapons and hard currency were carried overland to Vietnam via China. But in 1965, China began causing difficulties with this flow of supplies. At that time, he says, there was serious debate over whether or not to continue the struggle without Chinese support.

But the general is clearly anxious to begin his prepared lecture, and he indicates that the time for questions is over. He shuffles his papers. Why did the United States invade Vietnam, he begins. Vietnam is very small, with one-fifth the population of the United States. It is poor and far away. It shares with the United States a history of struggle against colonialism. It has never provoked the United States, and indeed, tried many times to establish good relations. He cites a number of letters written in the 1940s by Ho Chi Minh — including a proposal to set up a Vietnamese trust territory similar to the one governing the Philippines until 1946 — all of which went unanswered by the American government. But instead of treating Vietnam as a friend, he says, the United States entered into its longest and costliest war, flying in the face of world public opinion.

In fact, he says, from the U.S. government's point of view, there were three very good reasons to invade Vietnam. Firstly, Vietnam was the first Southeast Asian country to gain independence, and to allow one country to gain independence would send the wrong signal to other Third World countries. Secondly, Southeast Asia is historically important to U.S. global strategy: located at the center of Asia, it bridges the Pacific and Indian oceans; it is almost exactly halfway around the globe from the United States and almost equidistant between the poles. Thirdly, while Vietnam is small and poor, it is rich in resources; whoever controls Vietnam can exploit all of Indochina and the rest of Southeast Asia.

There were many excuses and pretexts given to justify American intervention, he says, but in reality it came down to those three things:

politics, geography and economics. Moreover, he adds, while the United States was defeated militarily, it has still not abandoned its attempts to occupy Vietnam and the rest of Indochina, a fact evident in the present hostility toward Vietnam on the part of successive postwar U.S. administrations, including the refusal of diplomatic recognition and normalization of relations, an economic embargo, and support for Vietnam's enemies, China and Pol Pot's Khmer Rouge.

What are the consequences of the American war, he asks, though it is not really a question. First is the division of the country and the misunderstandings between the Vietnamese people. As early as 2,000 B.C., Vietnam was an identifiable nation with a "national will" located in the Red River Delta in what is now northern Vietnam. Over the centuries, the Vietnamese migrated progressively southward, he tells us.

I know the history of the Vietnamese people already. And I know that the southward migration was still going on — the Vietnamese displacing the Cambodians in the extreme southern part of Vietnam around the Mekong Delta — when the French arrived in the middle of the 19th century and arrested the process by their own colonization. "Vietnamese imperialism?" I jot down in my notes, but I don't interrupt.

The French tried to divide Vietnam into three states, the general continues: Tonkin, Annam and Cochin, which together with Laos and Cambodia made up the five "provinces" of the French colony of Indochina. After many years, however, even the French had to recognize the unity of one Vietnam. The 1954 Geneva Convention ending the French Indochina War also recognized the unity of one Vietnam, and the division of the country at the 17th parallel was only supposed to be temporary. "Dividing Vietnam is like dividing a person," he says, gesturing with his hand as if quartering his own body. But the United States, through the puppets Bao Dai and Ngo Dinh Diem, tried to make the division permanent. This is the first U.S. crime.

The second U.S. crime, he continues, was the creation of hostility between and among the Vietnamese people themselves, dividing friends and families. Even before the Geneva Convention of 1954 was signed, the United States began to subvert it, sending spy teams and saboteurs into the north to spread false rumors and fake currency and to destroy public transportation and other vulnerable targets. Because of the false rumors and lies, nearly 1,000,000 Vietnamese Catholics moved south, destroying their homes and property and taking their wealth with them. These Catholics, he says, were deliberately resettled around important southern cities and military bases, making it impossible for the Viet Cong to attack the bases without attacking the Catholics. Catholic soldiers were used as shock troops and commandos, and they regularly looted the property of non–Catholic southerners.

At this point, the lights go out. A power failure, I wonder? It is 4:40 p.m. We have been at it for nearly four hours. It is terribly difficult to pay attention, or even to appear to be paying attention. It isn't that I don't believe what the general is saying. Political rhetoric and ideological theory aside, most of what he has said is true. The problem is that I am hearing almost nothing new. I already know about Ho's unanswered letters to Harry Truman. I already know that Colonel Edward Lansdale and his sabotoge teams destroyed the entire bus system of Hanoi in the summer of 1954, that northern Catholics were told by their priests and bishops that the Virgin Mary had fled to the south, that Ngo Dinh Diem — with the full support of the Eisenhower administration — refused to hold the reunification elections called for in the Geneva agreements. I've read enough books to fill a small public library. I don't need to hear this stuff again.

The lights come on again, but I ask for a break: I have been swilling tea all afternoon, and now my bladder is about to explode like an over-inflated balloon. The general decides to call it a day, telling us we will pick up tomorrow afternoon where we've left off. I can hardly wait, I think, hurrying down the hall as fast as I can without actually running.

John isn't feeling well and wants to lie down, but I've been cooped up all afternoon and I need some air and exercise. I suggest a walk to Bruce and Loan. It is dark outside, though the streets are still active. In a few blocks, we come to a public park with a large lake in the middle called Restoration Sword Lake. There are people strolling on the concrete sidewalk, and others sitting alone or in small groups on stone benches. Once, I catch a whiff of what smells like marijuana. I recall hearing that, at least in the south, marijuana was not illegal until the Americans arrived. It wasn't legal, either. It was just there, like dandelion. I don't remember now where I heard that, or if it is true, but certainly marijuana was prevalent enough when I was in Vietnam the first time. It was not unusual to see even old women smoking openly, and eventually marijuana became a major recreational pursuit of many American GIs. I've caught just a whiff, and then it is gone, and I do not ask if Bruce or Loan have smelled it, too. Perhaps I'm mistaken.

It is peaceful and very beautiful along the lake. The air is crisp and clean, and there is far less noise than in any American city. It's too dark to see clearly, and there are few lights to mark the lake's perimeter, but it appears to be quite large. Is it dangerous to be out alone at night, I ask. Oh, no, Miss Loan replies quickly. I remark that American cities can be very dangerous at night, that I seldom walk at night except in my own immediate neighborhood. No, it is very safe here, she replies. Sometimes there is domestic crime — family violence — but except for a burglary now and then, there is no real street crime.

We reach the far side of the lake and Miss Loan tells us this part of the city is called Old Hanoi. The streets are narrow and twisting — most of them no more than alleys — and the street life is rich and noisy and stimulating. Many small shops selling plastic sandals and cloth and china are still open, and street vendors ply pastries and fresh fruit and cigarettes. People sit on stoops and curbs cooking over small portable stoves, or squat in doorways watching and talking.

Loan asks if we want to eat *pho*, and takes us into a small shop — one is hard-pressed to call it a restaurant — with an open kitchen at the back consisting of a few pots and pans and a recessed cooking fire, and a few tables and benches toward the front. It is small — almost claustrophobic — dark, and crowded. Bruce, all 6 feet 4 inches of him, has difficulty wedging himself onto the bench between the wall and the table. For a moment, I wonder if we ought to be eating here: U.S. public health inspectors would probably drop dead of apoplexy at the very sight of a place like this. My doctor has given me dangerously powerful antidiarrhea pills, I remind myself without much comfort, should worse come to worst. But the *pho* is steaming hot and delicious, and I eat most of an enormous bowlful with a deep tin spoon and chopsticks before I have had enough.

Loan insists on paying for all three of us, and then we walk back to the hotel to get John. We are still not through for the day. Back at the ministry building, we are going to see a movie called *The First Love*. When we arrive, everyone is waiting for us except the general. The chairs have all been arranged along one side of the room, and a projector is set up and pointing toward the opposite wall. There is some difficulty with the projector, then additional difficulty with the speakers, but at last we get rolling. The film is in Vietnamese, so Mr. Quang and Loan must translate as we go.

As the film begins, we see a happy couple embracing beneath the spectacular waterfall near the city of Dalat. They are young and obviously in love. Soon, however, the woman ends up marrying an American doctor. Broken-hearted, the young man becomes a "Saigon Cowboy" — a street punk—joining a gang and turning to crime and drugs. He's not a bad fellow, really—he gives most of his ill-gotten money to his poor mother—but he just can't seem to get his act together. Meanwhile, the woman discovers that her American husband is planning to kidnap a planeload of Vietnamese children and take them to the United States. She seeks out her old boyfriend and tells him. Why did she marry the American in the first place, he wants to know. She explains that her father was deeply in debt to the doctor and couldn't pay; marrying him was the only way to discharge the debt. Her explanation comes just in the nick of time: it seems that her husband has poisoned her, and she dies in the arms of her boyfriend. Filled with new resolve, he goes to the American's house, thwarts the kidnap plan and avenges his lover by shooting the doctor dead, and then goes off to join the revolution.

In spite of contemporary political overtones and the overdone melo-drama—I didn't like *Love Story*, either—I recognize the basic outline of the plot as a common theme in Vietnamese culture: the woman who sac-rifices herself, often in degrading ways, for the benefit of her family, the ultimate good finally being served in spite of—perhaps because of—the terrible personal tragedy. It is an allegory for the nation and people of Vietnam, the central theme of Vietnam's great national epic, *The Tale of Kieu*, written by the master poet Nguyen Du in the late 18th century.

As the lights go on, I notice that Loan's eyes are damp. Everyone is eager to know if we liked the movie, and I am suddenly aware that this has been a very special occasion for them, quite out of the ordinary routine and probably arranged only with difficulty. They are trying to please us, I realize, trying to show us a good time. They want us to like them, and their country. For the first time since we've arrived, I find myself feeling something inside other than anger and disappointment at not being able to visit the places I had known.

Loan walks us back to the hotel, then gets on her unlighted bicycle and rides off down the dark, deserted street. The bar in the hotel lobby is still open. I buy a small bottle of Russian vodka, paying with a dollar bill, take three glasses and join Bruce and John at one of the tables. We are beginning to realize that everything one buys, except goods actually made in Vietnam, one pays for with U.S. currency rather than dong. John, who has been to Bulgaria and Romania, tells me that such is often the case in socialist countries; it is a way of obtaining hard foreign cur-rency. The official exchange rate, fixed by the government rather than a free market, is always much lower than the actual exchange rate should be. This, too, adds needed dollars to the treasury. Later, on my way up to the room — as if to confirm what John has been saying — the night clerk at the front desk quietly offers to exchange dong for dollars at the rate of 50 to 1, over three times the official exchange rate. It is clearly a private and unofficial offer.

Earlier in the day, I had gone back to my room to discover that the bed had been made and the mosquito net had been collapsed and folded against the wall. Now I find that the bed has been turned down and the mosquito net has been reopened. I lie down and begin reading a James Michener novel I've brought along, but it is set in Bucks County, Pennsylvania — where I spent my childhood and where Anne and I had lived for two years before moving to Philadelphia the previous summer — and it makes me homesick. I put it aside. There is a scratching sound at the window. I get up to investigate and find a small white cat trying to get into the room. As I approach, it scampers away across the second floor terrace outside the window and disappears into the darkness.

Wednesday, December 18

The mausoleum of Ho Chi Minh is an elegantly simple building rising from the middle of an enormous public square. From the outside, black-pillared and austere in the early morning light, it looks like a dark version of Lincoln's memorial in Washington, D.C., though I think it is modeled on Lenin's tomb in Moscow.

We are eight this morning: Troan, Hoang, Loan, the two drivers, John, Bruce and I. As a young, smartly dressed army officer approaches us, our hosts tell us we must leave our cameras in the car. At the head of a narrow red carpet that begins several hundred meters from the mausoleum's entrance, the officer arranges us carefully in two columns of four, taking up a position of escort at our right side. We begin our walk toward the tomb, the officer setting the pace, periodically politely but firmly correcting one or the other of us for walking too fast or too slow. As we get close to the tomb, the pace of our escort slows to a solemn funereal walk.

At last we reach the entrance, which is flanked by two armed guards standing at attention, and go inside. Up several flights of stairs, with an armed guard posted at attention at each landing, we enter the room where the body of Bac Ho — Uncle Ho — lies in a glass case flanked by four more armed guards and surrounded by a brass rail and walkway. Thin and frail-looking, as he appeared in life, the first president of the Democratic Republic of Vietnam is dressed in a simple tunic and trousers. His hands are folded across his stomach, and the thin gray strands of his beard lie softly on his upper chest. Dead since 1969, he looks as though he might wake up at any moment.

Thoughout Vietnam, Ho Chi Minh has been elevated to the level of a secular god. His photograph, his bust, his face are everywhere. To a foreign observer, it is almost as if no other soul ever contributed one iota to the cause of Vietnamese independence in the 20th century. What about his comrades and peers, I find myself frequently wanting to ask. But for the Vietnamese, Ho Chi Minh is without peer. It is a curious irony that the collective state seems to require an individual hero: Lenin in Russia, Mao in China, Ho in Vietnam.

Still, anyone familiar with Ho Chi Minh cannot help being deeply impressed by his lifelong singular commitment to Vietnamese independence as he perceived it. As a young man in 1919, using the name of Nguyen Ai Quoc — Nguyen the Patriot — he traveled to Versailles, hoping to meet with Woodrow Wilson. Wilson had brought the United States into the First World War under the rallying cry of his Fourteen Points — including self-determination for all peoples and nations — and Ho hoped to enlist Wilson's support for Vietnamese independence from the French. But Wilson refused him even an audience.

History is replete with missed opportunities. The skinny young dreamer not worthy of American attention moved on from Versailles to socialism and then to communism, becoming one of the most formidable revolutionary strategists the world has ever known. Through years of exile and prison, through three wars — against Japan, France and the United States — he never relinquished his goal of a unified independent Vietnam. Once, several years ago, I was a guest on a television talkshow during which the moderator denounced Ho as an opportunistic carpetbagger who longed for nothing so much as to have been born a Frenchman. Now, as I study the body of the man in front of me, I remember that assessment and marvel at the ability of intelligent human beings to distort reality in whatever bizarre ways are necessary to maintain our illusions.

We are permitted only a few minutes in the inner room, then we are quietly shown out. As we leave, I find myself looking back and wishing that Ho had lived to see his country reunified. One might argue with his ideology and his methods, but one cannot avoid the fact that this was a remarkable man. And indeed, in Vietnam, one does not have to be a Marxist-Leninist to revere him. During the war, we often came upon houses with small altars to Ho. The people in those houses were usually beaten and arrested, the houses often destroyed. We were told that Ho Chi Minh was a communist. No one ever told us that many Vietnamese, northerners and southerners alike, hold him in much the same esteem as we hold George Washington. How many Vietcong did our blundering ignorance produce?

Behind the mausoleum is a small park consisting of a few low French-style buildings, a pond, and a tiny two-story house that is clearly not French. The house is Ho Chi Minh's, occupied in 1945 and 1946 — until the French forced Ho's withdrawal from Hanoi — and again from 1954 until Ho's death. The first floor has no walls; it is an open-air conference room with a large table and a dozen chairs. On the second floor, more fully enclosed but still open and airy, are a bedroom and a sitting room. As a park guide throws pieces of bread into the pond, which are gobbled up in a feeding frenzy by several dozen large golden carp, he tells us that Ho often came here to feed the fish and reflect upon his thoughts. Then he recites one of the many poems Ho wrote during his life, the guide actually singing in the lovely way that poems are recited in Vietnamese:

> When I first came here the rice was still tender green.
> Now half the autumn harvest has already been brought in.
> Everywhere peasants' faces wear smiles of gladness,
> And the ricefields resound with songs of happiness.

Perhaps it was all a pose, I think, this life of simple austerity and self-denial. But I can't help thinking of the rich opulence of Monticello and Mount Vernon, of the $300,000 of new china Nancy Reagan bought for the White House because what was there already was deemed inadequate. I try to imagine Richard Nixon writing poetry.

On the way to our next appointment, the Kampuchean embassy, we stop by Chua Mot Cot — the one-pillared pagoda — symbol of the city of Hanoi. I've already seen its likeness on everything from the hotel restaurant's plates to the labels on Hanoi Bia — Hanoi Beer. True to its name, it is a small Buddhist temple built on one piling in the center of a small, square pond. At the peak of its roof is a glass circle, symbolizing the sun, held between two dragons: the royal sign of the emperor. Loan tells us that the temple was built in A.D. 1049. In 1049, William the Conqueror was still a boy in Normandy, and England still belonged to the Saxons. It would be another 443 years before Christopher Columbus would accidentally stumble upon the Bahamas on his way to China.

Westerners have long called the country of the Khmers Cambodia. More recently, one often finds it called Kampuchea. On Vietnamese maps, it is rendered Cam Pu Chia. All are only rough approximations of the Khmer name for their country. General Chi has told us that he would like us to go there during our stay in Vietnam, and he has scheduled us to visit the Kampuchean embassy to help arrange the trip. We are not too keen on going to Kampuchea — though we are interested, we have only 16 days and too much to see as it is. But as we have already seen, what we want to do seems of little importance. Our itinerary has clearly been determined long before our arrival. So we go to the Kampuchean embassy.

We are greeted by a young man — a second secretary, I think — who shows us into a quietly elegant sitting room where two women serve us warm Coca-cola without ice. I notice that it is bottled in Singapore. Quickly we discover that the secretary speaks only a little Vietnamese, and none of our hosts speak Khmer. The secretary doesn't speak English either, but he speaks some French. John understands a little French. What follows is a strange conversation that reminds me very much of the Abbott & Costello routine, "Who's on first?" This is all compounded by the fact that the secretary wants to know why we want to go to Kampuchea, what we would like to see, and who we would like to meet with — which is not easy to explain in *any* language, since the trip isn't our idea in the first place. Everyone spends a lot of time smiling awkwardly, scratching their heads, and stumbling over words in four languages strewn about the room like boobytraps.

It is Wednesday morning, and I haven't communicated with Anne since Sunday night when I called from Bangkok. We go to the post office to send telegrams. Mine says, "Arrived Hanoi safely. I love you." It must be block-printed on a special form, in triplicate, no carbons. It costs 300 dong — about $21.50 at the official rate. At first the woman overcharges me, giving me too little change. When she discovers her error, she apologizes profusely, clearly embarrassed. She takes out a large sheet of brown paper, a rubber stamp and an ink pad. She stamps one corner of the paper, adds a few figures and the word "Philadelphia" in pen, then tears off the stamped piece with a metal straight-edge. This is my receipt. It measures two inches by three inches. She will get perhaps 40 or 50 receipts from that one piece of rough brown paper.

We go next door to mail the postcards we have bought in the hotel lobby. The cards are photos of Hanoi poorly reproduced on lightweight paper not much heavier than the cover of a *Newsweek*. That they will withstand the rigors of a 12,000-mile trip through the mail seems questionable at best, but I will try anyway, sending one to Anne and one to my parents. The stamps have no glue on them. On tables in the lobby are small jars of glue, but there are no applicators. Loan takes a piece of paper from her purse, tears off a corner and folds it into a glue applicator. Without apology or apparent embarrassment, she demonstrates how to apply the glue, her deft gestures indicating simply: this is how it's done.

After lunch at the hotel, fortified with a few belts of Russian vodka, we return to the ministry building for another session with General Chi. I am much relieved when Mr. Hoang returns our passports and visas, which we'd left at the police station the previous day. Before we begin, the general asks if we have any questions. With some trepidation, we ask as politely as we can if it might be possible to forego our sidetrip to Kampuchea, explaining — truthfully — that it is not a matter of lack of interest, but a question of time. Perhaps, we suggest, the general could arrange some sort of briefing on Kampuchea here in Vietnam.

If the general is irritated by our request, he does not show it. He will look into it, he replies. In the meantime, it so happens that the Third Conference of Young Vietnamese Writers is taking place in Hanoi this very week and he thinks he can arrange our schedule so that we might at least put in an appearance. Perhaps, also, he adds, he might be able to arrange for us to meet Te Hanh, one of Vietnam's two most famous living poets, and other members of the Writers' Union. We would like that very much, we reply, realizing these things were not on our original itinerary. "I thought you might," he says through Mr. Quang, "since you are writers and poets yourselves."

Then he picks up the pile of notes in front of him, indicating that it is time to begin. Mr. Quang picks up his pencil and prepares to write. The general speaks only a sentence or two at a time as Quang takes notes in Vietnamese. Then Quang translates for us from his notes. Sometimes, Quang must ask the general a question, get some sort of clarification, before he translates. The process is laborious and taxing for everyone.

The third U.S. crime, the general begins, picking up where he'd left off the day before, is the massacre of the people. "Our soldiers could avoid U.S. weapons," he says, "but the people could not." He estimates that 5 million people were killed or wounded during the course of the war — 10 percent of the population — 75 percent of them civilians. He recites U.S. weaponry and tactics: napalm, CS gas, defoliants, "super bombs" weighing 7.5 tons each, cluster bomb units with a killing radius of 500 meters, B-52s, search and destroy missions, and free fire zones that caused the forcible dislocaton and relocation of the rural population of Vietnam.

The fourth U.S. crime, according to the general, is the social consequences of the war: prostitution and drug addiction, orphans and Amerasian children, chemically caused stillbirths and deformed babies, the breakdown of traditional family relationships, old people without children to care for them, widows who must raise their children alone, thousands of people still suffering the physical and psychological effects of arrest, torture and imprisonment. The United States has 2,000 people missing in action, he points out, but the Vietnamese have ten times 2,000: more than 200,000 Vietnamese are still missing and unaccounted for more than ten years after the war.

There are also environmental consequences, he continues: the destruction of villages, food, wildlife and forests, and the introduction of "American grass" — a tough rapid-growing grass sown by the Americans in defoliated areas to keep the jungle from returning, or to open up clear fields of fire, that is now difficult to get rid of and overrunning many areas in the south. Old mines and bombs still make it difficult and unsafe to farm in many areas. He estimates that there are 15,000 to 30,000 tons of unexploded ordnance still lying in the ground, along with 21 million bomb craters and 229 million artillery craters. In addition, massive defoliation has led to severe flooding and has increased the impact of heavy rains and typhoons.

Economically, he says, United States aid to the south retarded development of indigenous handicrafts and industry, reducing the southern economy to a service economy centered around prostitutes, pimps and cyclo drivers. Under the French, Vietnam exported a million tons of rice per year, but after 1960, southern Vietnam could no longer even grow enough rice to feed its own people and had to become a rice-importing nation. In the north, too, the war took its toll. He refers to the infamous comment widely attributed to General Curtis LeMay about bombing the Vietnamese back to the Stone Age (though apparently LeMay never said this), elaborating on the effects of U.S. bombing including the destruction of centers of science and industry and the destruction of the irrigation systems of 20 northern provinces.

As they had done the day before, the lights go out. It is 4:30 p.m. How I long for this to be over. Again, it is not that I disagree, but only that I feel like a graduate student being forced to repeat the sixth grade. The lights go on again, but the general calls a halt for supper. As we are leaving, he and Quang approach me. The general pulls the translation of my poem "Making the Children Behave" from his pocket, and points to it, saying something in Vietnamese. "The general thinks you already know what he has been talking about," says Quang.

It is the most remarkable and refreshing thing I have heard in days. I am actually stunned. Carefully, I try to formulate a reply. "One can never know enough," I say, "but yes, I have been studying the war for a long time." Quang translates. Then the general puts his arm around my shoulder and speaks. "He asks you to be patient," Quang says, "We will be finished this evening."

"When you hear the sound of songs," the general says later that evening, "you can forget the sound of bombs." With that introduction, we begin the evening's session with a kind of film anthology of regional traditional songs, stylized and orchestrated, called "Homeland Songs." The film is in color, and it shows scenes from each of the regions from which the songs come. Each song is sung by a different woman, young, very beautiful, and dressed in an *ao dai*, the traditional formal dress of Vietnamese women. When the film ends, the general explains that one of the women in the film, Ai Van, has won international prizes for her singing. He also points out that a Vietnamese artist recently won the Chopin prize for piano.

And then we begin again, this time focusing on the postwar period. "Our cadre and officials were trained for war," the general begins, "but now we must learn to rebuild." Though Vietnam is a small nation, he says, its resources and potential are enormous: 10 million hectares of land for trees and food; rich soil, adequate water and relatively good weather allowing three rice crops per year as well as potatoes, beans, sugar, coffee, tea, peppers and other foods; 7,000 kinds of trees, including 2,000 kinds of wood trees and 1,800 trees useful in medicine along with many kinds of fruit trees; tigers, elephants and other wildlife; 1,000 rivers capable of producing hydroelectric power; 3,000 kilometers of seacoast; 50 types of crabs, 440 types of shrimp, and over 1,000 kinds of fish; 50 kinds of minerals including coal, natural gas, oil, titanium, gold, mercury and tin.

About the time we get to the 50 different kinds of crabs, Bruce tries to ask a question, but the general waves him off. He is clearly in no mood for questions. I think of what he said to me as we were leaving in the afternoon. Perhaps he is as anxious as we are to be done with this.

The potential is rich, the general continues, but there are "many difficulties." Among them, he says, are the hostile attitude of the United States government, the expansionist policies of the Chinese, and an unlucky succession of natural disasters including two major typhoons in central Vietnam this year alone. He repeats what we have already heard about American hostility, then elaborates more fully on China.

Immediately after the war, he says, China withdrew all aid and its remaining specialists. In addition, China used the 1.2 million ethnic Chinese living in Vietnam for sabotage and subversion. Agents of the Chinese government spread false rumors among these ethnic Chinese, warning them to flee for their lives. This caused great disruption to the Vietnamese economy, he says. For example, of 150,000 ethnic Chinese coal miners in one northern province, all but 6,000 returned to China, and all 3,000 ethnic Chinese dockworkers at the port of Haiphong returned to China. Additional thousands of ethnic Chinese, having been stirred up, tried to flee but were turned back at the border by the Chinese government. Finally, China attacked Vietnam, he insists, first using "the Pol Pot clique" to attack in the south, then attacking directly across the northern border.

All of these arguments I have heard before, though they have received little attention in the western press. Few Americans have any knowledge at all of the Chinese community that has lived in Vietnam for centuries without ever relinquishing its language or cultural identity. Given the long history of hostility between Vietnam and China, is it so far-fetched to imagine that the Chinese government might try to make these people witting or unwitting accomplices in an ongoing struggle against Vietnam? How many Americans know of the deep and continuing relationship between the Chinese government and the murderous Khmer Rouge of Pol Pot? As I listen, I imagine how General Chi's arguments would be received by the members of the Perkasie Rotary Club; it doesn't require much imagination.

After liberation in the south, the general continues, the situation was chaotic. A billion-dollar-a-year false economy generated by the war collapsed overnight. There were shortages of food and fuel. Millions of people who had fled to the cities during the war had to be moved back to the countryside. The new regime had to determine what to do with all the prostitutes, drug addicts, and people who had worked for the "puppet government." And dealing with all of this has been made more difficult by the hostile schemes of the United States, China and Pol Pot, requiring, among other things, that Vietnam continue to maintain a large army, costing the Vietnamese money and manpower they can ill afford.

"But Ho Chi Minh told us," he says, "that we must rebuild Vietnam to be ten times more beautiful than before, and that is what we are doing." Though the achievements of the past ten years have been small, they are very important: building a good regime, abolishing exploitation, increasing food production, and developing gas and oil production. The population has increased at the rate of a million per year, but living conditions are still improving. In 1975, with a population of 48 million, per capita consumption of food was 250 kilograms a year, and half a million tons of rice had to be imported; in 1985, with a population of 58 million, per capita consumption is up to 300 kilos, and rice imports are down to 200,000 tons. The Vietnamese are building a natural gas refinery, and the giant Hoa Binh hydroelectric plant will be ready by 1987. Vietnam can now produce two million tons of cement per year, and in the near future that figure will rise to four million tons. Vietnam has 5,500 professors and assistant professors, 300,000 college students, and 600,000 high school students. "Of course," he concludes, "I have to say that we have a lot of work to do. But we will do it, step by step."

By the time General Chi finishes, it is very late. I am stuffed with statistics and dog-tired, still not fully recovered from jet lag or the complete reversal of my internal body clock: the time difference between Vietnam and the eastern United States is exactly 12 hours. We return to the hotel, where several Vietnamese are gathered around an old television set in the lobby, watching a Russian news broadcast with Vietnamese voice-over. One segment covers an antinuclear demonstration in Washington, D.C.; I can read the banners of the protesters, but I have no idea what the commentator is saying. Another segment seems to be showing the opening of a new building in Moscow. I am too tired to pay attention, and soon drift up to my room. Because I have not taken notes on our original agenda, I have no idea what we will be doing tomorrow. Who cares, I think to myself as I lie down; whatever's coming, it can't be any more grueling than what I've already endured.

Thursday, December 19

The Thong Nhat Hotel is only for foreign guests, and I wake up wondering who were the three Vietnamese men watching television in the lobby the previous night. Hotel employees with nothing much to do so late at night? Interpreter/guides catching the news after depositing their charges for the day? Maybe they were plainclothes cops, secret police. After all, this *is* a communist country where political freedom is viewed very differently than it is in the United States. I've heard it said back in the States that foreigners like me are constantly followed. Am *I* being watched, I wonder as I brush my teeth in front of the cracked mirror in my bathroom. A cracked two-way mirror? With the toothbrush still in my mouth, I grin broadly and wink at my image in the glass.

Come to think of it, I've sensed almost nothing at all like the descriptions I've read and heard from the Soviet Union and some of the Eastern European states. Oh, I've seen lots of soldiers, but except for the ceremonial guards at Ho's mausoleum, most of them have been unarmed, off-duty, strolling the streets or walking through the shops by ones and twos and threes like any other citizen of Hanoi. And the only police I've seen are traffic cops, posted at major intersections in an attempt to replace the old French traffic lights that long ago ceased to function, though they still stand on many corners like mysterious relics from another civilization. If I'm being followed, I certainly haven't been aware of it, though I haven't really been paying much attention and I probably wouldn't know what to look for anyway. Someone enters my room twice a day to make the bed, refill my water bottles, change the towel and adjust the mosquito net, but I've tried to check carefully and as far as I can tell, nothing of mine has been disturbed.

On my way down to breakfast, I poke my head into the small room next to the toilets that seems to be a kind of kitchen-lounge-bedroom for what we would call the chambermaids, though I've seen both men and women doing that job. Two women squatting on the floor look up from their bowls of rice as I give them a smiling "hello." They look at me, then giggle to each other and smile back. On the stairway, I pass two men in business suits. I've seen them before and I think they're Russian. I make eye contact with both of them and say hello as cheerily as I can, but they stare right through me, as if I did not even exist.

From the very first night, I have noticed that few of the hotel guests have anything at all to say to each other, or at least to us. Is it because of the language barrier? But as Crosby, Stills and Nash say, a smile is something everybody says in the same language, and I can't even get a smile out of most of my fellow guests. Is it because we're American? Do they distrust us? I have no way of knowing, but making eye contact and trying to get someone to respond with a greeting has become a kind of game. So far, I don't seem to be winning. John and Bruce are having no better luck.

John and Bruce are already eating breakfast. Bruce is saying that he doesn't want to visit the Hanoi Hilton, which John says is on our morning's itinerary. The Hanoi Hilton is the sarcastic nickname American pilots gave to the prison where many of them were kept during the war. I know when we go there, we will be told that American prisoners were treated "humanely." I know that what we will be told will bear no resemblance to the stories told by the prisoners who survived their ordeal. It is irritating at times, this facade of terminology and posturing. The accounts of U.S. pilots are too numerous and too vivid to have been fabricated: starvation, torture, physical and emotional deprivation. Why won't the Vietnamese admit it? Surely it would be understandable: these pilots were bombing their homeland, destroying their country, killing their people. It was a war. No one could reasonably expect the Vietnamese to treat downed American pilots as honored guests. It isn't the treatment that grates so much as it is the hypocrisy, the insistence on maintaining the myth of humane treatment.

Yet how did we treat *our* prisoners? Many an armed Viet Cong captured in the field never even made it to the rear alive. It was often of little use to try to tell a platoon of young soldiers who'd lost three of their buddies to mines and boobytraps in the previous week that the Geneva Convention on Prisoners of War required us to treat our captives humanely. Those lucky VC who did eventually make it to the rear alive were usually beaten—often brutally, if one might distinguish one kind of beating from another—many times before they arrived. And once they reached the rear, formal interrogation awaited them, often involving a wide variety of ingenious torture techniques. Eventually, most of those that still lived would be turned over to the South Vietnamese army or National Police.

Once, in 1967, after delivering several prisoners to the National Police headquarters at Hieu Nhon, I asked the American Marine advisor there what happened to the prisoners after the National Police got them. "You don't want to know," Sgt. Ford had replied, and that was all he was willing to say. We, at least, were obligated to pay lip-service to some crude semblance of adherence to the rules of warfare. Away from the prying eyes of the American news media and visiting Congressional delegations, the ARVN and the National Police were not.

And none of this included that vast category of people classified as detainees: unarmed civilians detained for questioning. Old men, old women, girls, young boys. They were explicitly *not* to be treated as prisoners of war, but as noncombatants. There was a whole different set of rules that was to apply to them. Yet to see them handled by any group of soldiers in the field, one would have had a hard time distinguishing them from actual guerrillas captured with weapons. In an environment where more often than not your enemy was mines and boobytraps planted by unseen phantoms in the night, "Guerrilla War" often came down to this:

> It's practically impossible
> to tell civilians
> from the Vietcong.
>
> Nobody wears uniforms.
> They all talk
> the same language,
> (and you couldn't understand them
> even if they didn't).
>
> They tape grenades
> inside their clothes,
> and carry satchel charges
> in their market baskets.
>
> Even their women fight;
> and young boys,
> and girls.

It's practically impossible
to tell civilians
from the Vietcong;

after awhile,
you quit trying.

And anyone who persisted in trying was either a new guy or a gook-lover, in either case a person to be shunned and distrusted. Meanwhile, detainees, too, were regularly turned over to the National Police.

To my knowledge, little of this has ever been officially admitted by the United States government or any agency thereof. There may have been "excesses" from time to time, an occasional isolated incident — so the official version goes — but such treatment was surely neither routine nor condoned. But just as I have read the accounts of captured American pilots, I have read the accounts of dozens and even hundreds of other former soldiers like myself. Moreover, I know what I did and what I saw. Is the disparity between official "fact" and unofficial reality really any different from the one we are about to be confronted with during our visit to the Hanoi Hilton?

Our first stop of the morning isn't the prison, however, but rather the Hanoi Committee of Solidarity and Friendship with Other Peoples. We are served tea, peanuts, tangerines and bananas, along with Vietnamese cigarettes. Repeated attempts to discover what the committee actually does are met with repeated explanations that sound like endless variations on the committee's name. Like a Pachelbel canon in Vietnamese, I think to myself. Are they being deliberately vague, or is something being lost in translation? I do manage to gather that they've all seen me in Episode 5 of the 1983 PBS series *Vietnam: A Television History*. Most of the rest of the visit I spend peeling tangerines and wondering why I bothered eating breakfast.

At the Vietnam-U.S. Society, we encounter more tea, bananas and peanuts, this time accompanied by small glasses of Vietnamese lemon liquor with which we toast the friendship of the people of Vietnam and the progressive American people. The society, we are told, is one of 36 bilateral societies included under the umbrella of the Vietnam Friendship and Solidarity Committee. Other than that, I learn little more than I did about the Hanoi Committee of Solidarity and Friendship with Other Peoples. I try to follow Loan's translation of the explanation, but there is nothing to latch onto but those nebulous, jello-like generalities.

I'm beginning to think that the failure to understand must be my fault—I'm still not fully recovered from jet-lag, and finding it difficult to sleep without Anne—when the man next to me suddenly says, "I've read some of your poems. I like them very much." He says it in English. I almost fall out of my chair.

"Where have you seen my poems?" I ask.

"I have a copy of *Winning Hearts and Minds*," he replies—a 1972 anthology of poetry published under the sponsorship of Vietnam Veterans Against the War.

"Where'd you get that?" I ask.

"Oh, I read quite a lot of American literature," he says, "I admire your writers very much. My favorites are Mark Twain, William Faulkner and Ernest Hemingway."

His name is Do Xuan Oanh. As we talk, I learn that he was once a coal miner, the son and grandson of coal miners. He has never had any formal education, but he is fluent in English, French and Chinese, and speaks conversational Russian as well. In English, at least, he is clearly not only fluent, but idiomatic. Once a member of the north Vietnamese delegation to the Paris Peace Talks in the late 1960s and early 1970s, he is a musical composer and translator. Months later, I will hear that to the wives and families of American POWs and MIAs who came to Paris during the war, he was perceived as the epitome of cold-blooded callousness. But here on his own turf, years later, he is charming and witty. As we talk, I suddenly realize how relaxed and at ease I feel, and what an enormous strain it is to carry on shallow conversations via rough-hewn and confusing translations.

"I hope your country appreciates you," he says as we leave, "Your poems speak from the heart. The whole world is much in need of men who speak from the heart."

"And women, too," I say, laughing.

"Yes, yes, of course, and women, too. Oh, I've blown my cover, haven't I? Now you will think me a male chauvinist."

It is not yet 10 a.m., but already we are off to our third stop of the morning: Bach Mai Hospital. Bach Mai Hospital may well be one of the most famous hospitals in the world. It was bombed by B-52s during the so-called "Christmas bombing" of 1972. The Vietnamese say the bombing of Bach Mai was deliberate. The United States government says it was an accident—and many Americans even deny that the hospital was bombed at all, though eyewitness and photographic evidence would seem to be conclusive. In any case, the bombing of Bach Mai became an international rallying cry for those opposed to the war, and the hospital became famous.

We are met by Dr. Luong Sy Can, director of the Ear, Nose and Throat Clinic, a 130-bed adjunct to the main 1,000-bed hospital. As we go through the ritual of tea and tangerines—for the first time, there are no Vietnamese cigarettes on the table, perhaps in deference to the medical risks of smoking—Dr. Can tells us that he was trained in Hanoi, France and Hungary. His daughter is a doctor, and his son also works in a hospital. He knows friends of mine—John McAuliff, who helped us arrange this trip, and Dave Elder of the American Friends Service Committee. He even stayed in Philadelphia, only a few blocks from my home, the previous summer during a medical tour of the United States. He is one of the few Vietnamese that have been allowed into the country by the United States State Department. In 1985, over 400 Americans were granted visas by the Vietnamese government. During the same period, 10 Vietnamese were granted visas by the United States.

Later, as we tour the hospital, I am amazed by how dirty and shabby it is. Patients wearing their own clothes rather than hospital gowns lie on beds covered with thin straw mats instead of mattresses. Many of the patients are accompanied by other family members who sit on the beds or squat nearby on the floor. I have to keep reminding myself that this isn't Doylestown Memorial Hospital, but a hospital in a very poor country in the Third World.

Dr. Can shows us several modest laboratories with microscopes and other equipment, some of it being used by young medical technicians. In one room, a nurse is testing a young girl's hearing with equipment donated by Sweden. In another room are several X-ray machines, gifts of the West German government. "We need so much," Dr. Can sighs, "We have almost nothing." In a small classroom, a young woman is teaching deaf children how to speak. Next door, two men are working on several pieces of electronic equipment. "We fix most things right here," says Dr. Can, "We can't afford to throw anything away."

Dr. Can takes us through several empty operating rooms, explaining that the surgical staff of 30 performs four to six major operations each day, along with numerous minor ones. He opens another door, and suddenly we are in an operating room in the midst of an operation. I think of all the sterilization precautions taken in U.S. hospitals—and here we are, barging in right off the street—but Dr. Can motions us toward the table. A woman is having a tumor removed from her throat. Acupuncture needles stick out of her body at various points. They are her only anesthetic. I feel slightly nauseated and remain at the edge of the room, leaning against the wall.

Outside, built against one wall of the hospital, is a memorial to the victims of the Christmas bombing. "If the Americans had wanted to bomb the hospital," I ask Dr. Can as we stand looking at the memorial, "Wouldn't they have leveled the whole place?"

"That may be true," he replies, "but it means nothing to those who died."

Loan interrupts, explaining that we are expected at the Vietnamese Young Writers' Conference and we are already late. We arrive at the cultural center at 11:45 a.m. and are shown into a large auditorium packed with several hundred people. Bruce, John and I are immediately ushered on stage and introduced to much applause.

"What are they saying about us?" I ask John.

"I'll be damned if I can follow it," he replies with a sheepish shrug.

"Read your poem," Loan says, nudging me.

"What?!" I reply, incredulous.

"Read your poem," she repeats, taking out her copy of the translation of "Making the Children Behave."

"But it's in Vietnamese."

"No," she laughs, "you read it in English, then I'll read it in Vietnamese."

"But I don't have an English-language copy," I protest.

"Fake it," says John, grinning.

It is a short poem and I manage to render it fairly accurately, realizing even as I'm speaking that it doesn't make much difference since nobody here can understand what I'm saying anyway. When Loan finishes reading the translation, we get a standing ovation. I wonder if I'm the first American ever to give a poetry reading in Hanoi. No, I think, Denise Levertov probably did it back in the sixties, back when I thought that Americans who went to Hanoi were traitors.

What happened to the Hanoi Hilton, I wonder aloud as Bruce, John and I eat lunch later back at the hotel, grateful for a break in what is proving to be a killing pace. We conclude that the prison visit must have been scuttled in favor of the writer's conference. Already the rigidly planned itinerary seems to be changing, as if General Chi and his staff are really trying to accommodate these three strange people who've come to complicate their lives. John mentions that Loan has told him the war crimes commission has never hosted American visitors before.

"I don't think we're quite what they expected," I say. Perhaps, as John and Bruce had suggested on our first night, things really will get better as we go along.

In the afternoon, we drive to the edge of the city to visit the Nguyen Viet Xuan Orphanage School. Founded in 1969, it is named for a young artilleryman killed in 1964 by American bombers. A photo of Nguyen Viet Xuan hangs on one wall of the reception room where we meet Le Duy Ai, director of the school. Like everywhere else we go, Ho Chi Minh's portrait hangs on another wall, in this case flanked by portraits of Lenin and Karl Marx.

The orphans here, like all orphans in Vietnam, are "Uncle Ho's children," Mr. Ai tells us over tea, bananas and sweet cookies very much like American sugar wafers while I wonder why I bothered eating lunch. The school has 400 children aged 7 to 17 in grades 1 through 12. There are 60 teachers. Here the children have a home; they receive an education and are taught a trade. All of the children are war orphans, he explains, from the United States war and from the Chinese border war.

What happens to orphans who are not war orphans, we ask. "What do you mean?" he replies through Loan. Children whose parents die of disease or in accidents, we explain. He still doesn't seem to understand. Is he obtuse, or is Loan not translating properly? Finally, after repeated questioning, we are told that "they are taken care of elsewhere." Additional questions fail to reveal where "elsewhere" is.

What will happen to the school when all the children are grown, we ask. Mr. Ai looks puzzled as Loan translates. When the children grow up and there are no more war orphans, we ask again, what will you do with the school? Mr. Ai listens to the translation, then confers in Vietnamese with Loan, Mrs. Troan and Mr. Hoang. God only knows what the confusion is, but for all the world it *appears* as if Mr. Ai cannot imagine a time when there will be no more war orphans. Is this what 30 years of war does to a country, I wonder, or does Mr. Ai know something about the future that I don't, or what? Mr. Ai lights a cigarette, offers the pack to us, then explains the various kinds of vocational training the school offers.

We finish our tea and take a tour of the school. One class is studying biology. Another is learning how to sew: girls and boys huddle over a dozen machines powered by manual footplates, no electricity required. Mr. Ai explains that the sewing machines are the private gift of a woman from Italy. As we watch the children working — they are making clothing that the orphans themselves will wear — there takes place what is clearly an awkward and embarrassing exchange between one of the students and his teacher. Loan doesn't want to tell me what it's about, but I press her. "His parents were killed by American bombers," she finally says with evident discomfort, "He wants to know why we would allow Americans to come to this school."

"Sounds like a fair question to me," I reply. I don't need to ask what the teacher's response has been. I'd be willing to bet a 100-pound bag of rice that the boy has just received a quick refresher course in the difference between the imperialist American government and the progressive American people. And though there may not be quite so many progressive American people as folks here seem to think, the explanation isn't entirely without merit.

From the school, we drive to a small factory that repairs radios and televisions and manufactures electrical transformers and electric fans. The director of the factory is Ngo Thi Thanh Thuc, a sturdy and jovial woman in her late forties with a master's degree in electrical engineering. As we sip tea and eat peanuts and more sugar cookies—it is no use trying to explain that we're full—Mrs. Thuc explains that the factory was founded in 1978. All 200 employees are either war invalids or graduates of the Nguyen Viet Xuan Orphanage School. They are paid slightly higher wages than ordinary factory workers receive, she says, one of the ways the state tries to take care of the disadvantaged.

After a brief tour of the factory, which reveals that most of the work is done by painstakingly slow manual labor, Mrs. Thuc invites us to join her and her staff for dinner. Can we do that, we ask Loan. Mrs. Troan and Mr. Hoang are beaming. "Yes, all of us will," says Loan, "It is a little surprise for you." We pile into our cars and take off for parts unknown, this time followed by two cars full of people from the factory. On the outskirts of town, we pass a number of more or less new high-rise apartment complexes, some occupied, others still under construction. The architecture reminds me of films I've seen of Russia: "Koncreteblocksnograd."

Horns blaring all the way, we arrive at the Thang Long Hotel about dusk. It is newer than the Thong Nhat Hotel, where we are staying. It's name means "Rising Dragon," the ancient name for the city of Hanoi. Inside, in a special banquet room, we are served an incredible meal of beef, salad, carp, eel soup, crab, pork, pigeon soup and chicken—each course served one at a time by a middle-aged man in a tuxedo and a young woman in a yellow and white *ao dai*. Rice comes with everything, and the meal is washed down with a seemingly endless supply of Vietnamese "33" Beer. As we eat, it occurs to me that probably no one at this table eats this way very often, that this is probably as much of a treat for our hosts as it is for us. I am delighted to be able to provide them with a good excuse. There are numerous toasts to peace and friendship, punctuated by glasses of *lua moi*, a potent Vietnamese vodka made from rice.

The man sitting next to me, one of Mrs. Thuc's assistants, is missing his right arm from the shoulder. His name is Nguyen Van Hung, and he is 38 years old. As we talk, Mr. Hung and I discover that both of us fought in Hue City during the bloody Tet Offensive of 1968. The more we talk, the more a kind of brotherhood of adversaries takes root between us.

"You weren't a B-40 gunner, were you?" I ask with a laugh, wondering if by some bizarre coincidence this might be the man who had wounded me.

"No," he replies, "I was with the special units. I was a sapper" — a demolitions engineer.

Why am I so attracted to this man? I lost so many friends to men like him. But then, how many friends did he lose to men like me? It was all so long ago, and we were very young. Here at last is a direct link with my own past. This guy was there, I think to myself, this guys knows what it was like.

"Did you lose your arm in Hue?" I ask.

"No," he explains, "I lost it near the Laotian border in 1971." My war lasted 13 months. His lasted until he was physically dismembered. He smiles at me, fascinated by my ability to roll cigarettes by hand, and asks me to roll one for him. He pours us each another glass of *lua moi*. When the evening ends, he takes my hand and squeezes it. "I'm glad you weren't killed," he says. He breaks into a broad, toothy grin, and I embrace him with both arms, happy that both of us have lived to share this moment.

Friday, December 20

During the 80-odd years of French colonial rule, the emperor of Vietnam was little more than a figurehead with no real political power. Indeed, Bao Dai, the last hereditary emperor, who came to the throne at age 12 upon the death of his father in 1925, spent the next seven years in France, living in the home of a French civil servant while receiving a French education. Upon his return to Vietnam, he was more frequently to be found hunting, dining and womanizing than he was to be found performing his official duties, limited though these were.

Still, he embodied for many Vietnamese "the mandate of heaven" that had passed from emperor to emperor for centuries. Thus, it was no empty gesture when in August 1945, Bao Dai abdicated his throne and publicly acknowledged allegiance to Ho Chi Minh, president of the newly declared Democratic Republic of Vietnam, though he would soon change his mind when things began to go badly for Ho and the Viet Minh—as he had changed his mind with regard to the Japanese during World War Two—returning to the French fold later in the French Indochina War and finally ending up as the first head of state of the Saigon-based southern Republic of Vietnam before finally being ousted in 1955 by the American client, Ngo Dinh Diem. A leaf in the wind, his life was a sad conclusion to an ancient lineage.

During our morning meeting with representatives of the Central Committee for Vietnamese Culture, Literature and the Arts, cultural folk art specialist Bui Van Nguyen tells us that the house we are in, originally built during the French occupation, was the home of Bao Dai during the year he spent as "senior advisor" to Ho Chi Minh in 1945 and 1946. After Bao Dai withdrew his allegiance and fled Hanoi, the house was given to Vietnam's artists by the government. "Artists are the new kings of Vietnam," says the professor, smiling. It reminds me of John Keats's assertion that "poets are the unacknowledged legislators of the world." Wouldn't it be nice if it were true, I find myself thinking. But then, Robert Frost was supposedly a crusty old curmudgeon, and Ezra Pound was a raving antisemite and open admirer of Mussolini. Would it really be a better world if poets were in charge?

John explains his interest in *ca dao*, Vietnamese oral folk poetry. To the obvious delight of our hosts, he recites in Vietnamese several of the *ca dao* he recorded and translated in the early 1970s. "Here is a soldier's *ca dao*," Professor Nguyen says when John has finished, explaining that it is newer than most, probably dating from the siege of Dien Bien Phu:

> If you don't have a vehicle to pull the artillery,
> you must use your shoulders:
> one shoulder to pull the gun,
> one shoulder to bring the moon.

After our morning meeting, our entourage goes to Restoration Sword Lake to visit Jade Hill Pagoda. The pagoda stands on a small island in the center of the lake, connected to the shore by a graceful footbridge called Sunshine Bridge. It was built in honor of Tran Hung Dao, a 13th century Vietnamese general who defeated Chinese invaders. The lake itself—sometimes rendered in English as the Lake of the Returned Sword—derives its name from a legend involving the repulse of yet another Chinese invasion. China has invaded Vietnam numerous times in the past four millennia, at one point occupying Vietnam for nearly a thousand years. More recent intrusions by France, Japan and the United States are mere aberrations in the great sweep of Vietnamese history.

"China is our natural enemy," General Chi had told us at one point in his lectures—and the imposition of communist governments in both countries has not altered that ancient antagonism, as the ongoing border war between the two countries attests. As we stand in front of Tran Hung Dao's shrine, I wonder at the utter ignorance of the educated people at the center of power who dragged the United States into the quagmire of Vietnam. If only American policymakers had taken the time to learn what every Vietnamese schoolchild knows, how different for both our countries might have been the course of the past 40 years.

"What does it say?" I ask Loan, pointing to the words chiseled on the shrine.

"'If you want to serve your country, take care of the common people,'" she replies, explaining that these supposedly were Tran Hung Dao's dying words.

For lunch, John, Bruce and I decide to forego the hotel restaurant — the limited menu of which is beginning to get a little boring — in favor of a walk through Old Hanoi. We are startled to come upon several old pagodas in back alleys that are now being used as simple residences. They are so old, so rundown, and so crowded in by the buildings around them, that we almost miss them entirely. How long have they been here, I wonder; when did they cease to be active temples? But there is no way to tell.

Everywhere we go, we are regularly taken to be Russians. *Lien Xo*, people say as we pass. When we respond, *My* — American, reactions range from befuddlement to giggles to broad smiles of appreciative amazement. Few northerners have ever seen Americans, and many of them, I suspect, are wondering where are our tails and horns. We stop, finally, to eat at a little hole-in-the-wall much like the one Loan took Bruce and me to earlier in the week.

We've only been subjected to one ritual dose of tangerines and bananas this morning, and we are all hungry: having grown accustomed already to multiple snacks throughout the day, our stomachs don't quite know what to make of this sudden deprivation. All of the other patrons seem to be eyeing us furtively — not in a hostile way, but with evident curiosity — but they are much too polite to ask us who we are. John trots out his best Vietnamese, but he can't seem to get the proprietor to understand what we want. Finally, a man sitting alone at another table gets up and approaches us.

"Do you need help?" he asks in halting English. We explain as best we can, then he says something in Vietnamese to the proprietor, who disappears into what must be the kitchen. The man, who is middleaged, lingers for a moment, as if wanting to say something more, then bows slightly and returns to his table. Our food soon arrives, and by the time we are finished eating, the man who has come to our rescue is gone.

On our way back to the hotel, we pass by a corner of Restoration Sword Lake where half a dozen older women are cleaning the park. Armed only with crude short-handled straw brooms, they are making a clean sweep of everything in sight, sweeping not only the concrete walks but also the broad expanse of grass as well. I have never seen anyone sweeping a lawn before. I try to imagine a brigade of matrons sweeping their way through Philadelphia's Fairmount Park, and burst out laughing. A block further on, we pass a construction site where a man carries bricks using half a 55-gallon drum for a hod while two other men laboriously cut their way lengthwise through a massive wooden beam with a hand-held double-handled crosscut saw.

In the afternoon, our entourage drives to the Fine Arts Museum. It is housed in a huge French-style building that must have been more than elegant once upon a time, though like most other buildings in Hanoi, it appears to be well past its prime. Inside are exhibits of arts and crafts from among the 60 tribal minority peoples living within Vietnam. Many of these tribal minorities remained in the Stone Age right up to and even during the American war.

Like native Americans in the 17th, 18th and 19th centuries, the indigenous tribes were not so much absorbed by the southward moving Vietnamese as they were simply brushed aside, driven from the fertile coastal lowlands up into the inhospitable highlands and mountainous regions. The French called them montagnards — mountain people — and the American CIA and the Green Berets tried to forge them into an indigenous army of resistance. No doubt, in many areas, the communists tried to do the same thing. Many tribes were utterly devastated by this sudden violent intrusion of the 20th century, and their histories are among the very saddest of all the victims of the Indochina wars. The current regime stresses that it respects the integrity and cultural identity of its tribal minorities, and has ongoing programs designed for their benefit. I wonder if Vietnam's indigenous peoples are making out any better than our own native Americans.

In other galleries are exhibits of Vietnamese art: paintings and sculptures, mostly. Not surprisingly, much of it is what we might call "combat art": a sculpture of a determined man bending over a machine-gun, a large and strikingly beautiful oil painting of a Viet Minh patrol crossing a mountainous ridgeline at dusk, a smaller watercolor of a duel between an artillery battery and a U.S. F-4 Phantom fighter-bomber. The galleries are poorly lit, with only a bulb in each corner high up near the ceiling, probably reflecting both the preciousness of electricity and the scarcity of lightbulbs.

From the museum, we go to the Van Mieu Pagoda — the Temple of Literature. Vietnam's first university, founded in A.D. 1077, it operated continuously for eight centuries. Now it is preserved as a museum and cultural shrine. "Literature is as necessary as the sunshine," the middle-aged woman curator says. "On that balcony there, the poets used to come to read their poems to the people." The balcony overlooks a reflecting pool surrounded by numerous upright slabs that look like oversized gravestones. Each stone stands on the back of a stone turtle, the symbol for long life. The curator explains that each marker is engraved with the names of that year's graduating class of students, together with the names of the students' examiners.

All around me are dozens of stones representing thousands of graduates over hundreds of years. The stone I am looking at, the curator tells me, is 770 years old. Others are even older. Back home where I grew up in Bucks County, Pennsylvania, it was an exciting occasion to encounter a covered bridge that was 80 years old, or a house that had been built before the American Revolution.

Inside the temple itself, the curator explains to us that the Vietnamese never lost their distinct cultural identity, even during the long occupation of the Chinese from 111 B.C. to A.D. 939. By the 12th century, the Vietnamese had developed their own written language, called "nom." Though to my eyes, it looks like Chinese, she assures me that it would be unintelligible to a Chinese person. *Nom* flourished well into the 17th century, until a Portuguese missionary developed the romanized alphabet still used today, and could still be found in use well into this century.

The curator glances nervously at her watch, then explains that she must cut our visit short. Her husband is a soldier stationed along the Chinese border; she lives alone with her two children, and she must get home in time to meet her children after school. Then she reaches into her pocket and comes up with three small enamel pins bearing the likeness of the Poets' Balcony. She hands one to each of us. "I want you to have these," she says. "When the Americans were here before, they bombed us. I'm glad you've come to the Temple of Literature. I'm very glad to meet you."

"Do you remember the bombing?" I ask Loan as she pins the curator's gift to my lapel.

"Yes," she replies, "It was terrible." She explains that she and most other children of Hanoi were evacuated to the countryside in 1965. She was five then, and for the next seven years she lived with her grandparents, seeing her parents only once each week. "We were close enough to hear the sirens and the guns and the bombs exploding," she says. "When the raids finally stopped, we were so happy that we ran all the way back to the city."

Later, in front of the ministry building, Loan tells us that we are finished for the day; the evening is ours. "You must be very tired," she says, "It's been a busy week." Mrs. Troan, Mr. Hoang and our drivers all wave and smile as we cross the street toward the hotel. I wonder what happened to the Military Museum we were supposed to have visited, but it occurs to me that our hosts must be as weary as we are. Today's schedule has been much less hectic than yesterday's, and the planned itinerary is proving to be less inflexible than I had feared. Whether the changes are in response to us and our perceived needs and interests, or to their own discovery that the schedule they've planned is murderously paced, I don't know.

Probably, it is a combination of both. Certainly, it has become clear that they *are* trying to schedule activities that will introduce us to the culture of Vietnam as much as to the politics of the war, activities I don't recall hearing much about during the general's original rundown of our itinerary. The Hanoi Hilton was dropped from yesterday's schedule, and now today the Military Museum. The Writers' Conference was added, and I think the Temple of Literature was not on our original agenda.

Over the course of the week, in fact, we and our entourage have gotten to know each other better, and they have warmed up considerably. Mrs. Troan, always polite but initially very reserved, has gotten into the habit of reciting poems in Vietnamese to John, eager to share what she feels is a common bond, and while Bruce and I cannot understand her, it is strangely moving to watch her animated face and listen to her high-pitched melodic voice. Mr. Hoang, straight-faced and aloof for the first few days, is constantly stuffing Vietnamese cigarettes into our mouths. Only today, our driver produced a bag of strong, dark Lao tobacco less than an hour after John had asked whether or not he'd ever encountered it in Hanoi, and he wouldn't let us pay for it. And Loan has begun to share with us slightly off-color jokes that delight and embarrass her simultaneously. She's been especially playful about John's purchase of a bottle of alcohol called "Gecko Elixir," which she tells us—with much difficulty and giggling—is supposed to increase one's sexual potency.

The free evening, however, is a mixed blessing. The magnitude of my homesickness—the passion of my longing for Anne, really—startles and frightens me. I had expected to miss her. I had not expected this brief separation to be so very painful. I suspect that John and Bruce, at first amused, are beginning to find it tedious. In any case, in a way I have been grateful for the breakneck pace we've been keeping because the busier I am, the less time I have to sit around worrying about Anne. As I had once done as a scared young Marine, I find myself constantly counting days until I can go home.

Moreover, much as we like each other, all three of us are discovering that for all the years we've known each other, we really don't know very much about each other beyond our poetry. We are now discovering that I complain too much, that Bruce takes too long in the bathtub, that John is eating all the aspirin. We have been thrown together in very close quarters in a situation of unusual stress thousands of miles from home, and we have no one else to talk to but each other, and I don't want to be around them so much, and I don't want to be alone.

I walk over to Restoration Sword Lake and sit in the darkness watching the water. Hanoi, I think: it is almost unreal to be here. What was it like during the bombing? I have seen photographs of the mobile anti-aircraft units firing up at the sky from street corners, the hundreds and even thousands of one-person bombshelters built right into the sidewalks, the sandbagged buildings with their wire-covered windows—but in 1985, not a trace remains to be seen. An old man shuffles by with a small boy in hand. Both stare at me momentarily as they pass, but they don't stop.

What is it like now in Hue, in Danang and Quang Tri and Hoi An? The pain of my disappointment rises up more strongly than it has in days, and I get up and begin walking just to have something to do. I pass what seems to be a bar. There is rock and roll music coming from inside, a tape probably, but I cannot place the musicians—perhaps Japanese or Swedish or Australian. For a moment, I consider going inside. Not tonight, I think, I am too tired to deal with the strain of trying to communicate without a common language.

Back at the hotel, I buy a glass of lemon liquor from the bar and sit down in the lobby. Several men—perhaps Algerian or Palestinian—are sitting at one of the other tables in the otherwise empty lobby. One of them makes eye contact with me, and I smile and he nods in reply. Hey, maybe I'm finally getting somewhere, I think. But he turns back to his conversation, and that is the end of that. The television is on, showing a documentary about the army. Our trip happens to coincide with the 41st anniversary of the founding of the army. I notice the brand name on the television, which is written in English: "Friendship."

Saturday, December 21

General Chi is waiting with the others in the ministry building courtyard. It is the first time we've seen him since Wednesday. He greets us warmly and apologizes for his long absence. Explaining that he has arranged to travel to Ho Chi Minh City with us, he tells us he is having to work very hard in order to get caught up before we leave.

This morning, in lieu of a trip to Phnom Penh, the general has arranged for us to meet with Nguyen Phu Soai, deputy director of the International Relations Institute, who will give us a briefing on Kampuchea. Over coffee, tea and tangerines, Mr. Soai tells us — through an interpreter from the institute — that he is a native southerner and former guerrilla fighter, one of the founders of the Viet Cong forces in Quang Ngai Province. Like General Chi, however, he is reluctant to offer more than the bare minimum of personal details. Almost immediately, he begins his discussion of Kampuchea.

From the beginning, Mr. Soai tells us, Pol Pot was acting as an agent and puppet of China: the problems with Kampuchea since the liberation — meaning the end of the Vietnam war in the spring of 1975 — are only a reflection of Chinese expansionism; well before liberation, having failed to control Vietnam, China turned to Pol Pot. This is only one aspect of China's policy of aggression. After liberation, China also tried to exploit Vietnamese difficulties by inciting ethnic Chinese living in Vietnam, as well as Vietnamese from the old "puppet regime." Finally, when all else failed, China instigated military attacks along the Vietnamese-Chinese border.

For his part, according to Mr. Soai, Pol Pot first used the Vietnamese to fight the Americans, then turned on Vietnam once the United States was defeated. Pol Pot's aggression against Vietnam, in the form of border raids in and around Tay Ninh Province, began almost immediately after liberation. For three years, he says, Vietnam tried to negotiate a peaceful solution. In 1976, there were even summit talks between Pol Pot and Vietnam's first secretary, Le Duan. When Pol Pot unilaterally broke off these discussions, the Vietnamese tried to negotiate through intermediaries. All discussions failed, says Mr. Soai, because Pol Pot and his Chinese sponsors were not interested in finding a peaceful solution.

If all three countries are communist, we ask, why did Pol Pot and China want to attack Vietnam?

Some countries, he replies, use Marxist-Leninist theory to disguise their own self-interest. There must be a proper balance between patriotism and cooperation, between nationalism and internationalism. In Vietnam, the Party teaches internationalism. "We believe in a policy of good neighbors," he says, explaining that for more than three years Vietnam refused to be provoked by Pol Pot's attacks, but instead tried repeatedly to find the path to harmony. "We were very patient," he says. "Even when Pol Pot was killing our people, we believed we could find a peaceful solution."

Was it Pol Pot's genocide that finally forced Vietnam to act, we ask.

No, he explains, the Vietnamese did not know the extent of the genocide until after Vietnamese troops had entered Kampuchea. They had heard reports from Western sources, but they thought these reports were just propaganda. "Later, we recognized this was a mistake on our part," he says, "but how could we believe it then? Pol Pot had been our wartime ally, our friend. Who could believe a man could do such a thing to his own people?"

Then why did Vietnam invade Kampuchea?

"Oh, we did not invade Kampuchea," he replies quickly. Only when Pol Pot rejected every offer to negotiate and instead attacked Vietnam in December 1978 with 19 divisions of soldiers did Vietnam finally take up arms. "Then we had no choice," he says. "It was a full scale invasion of our homeland. We had to defend ourselves."

But Vietnamese soldiers marched all the way to Phnom Penh, we point out; they occupied all of Kampuchea.

The Vietnamese did not set out to overthrow Pol Pot, he replies, but only to defend Vietnam's borders. Once Vietnam defeated the Pol Pot attack, the Kampucheans themselves overthrew "the Pol Pot clique."

But there are 100,000 Vietnamese troops in Kampuchea, we say; isn't it they who overthrew Pol Pot?

Of course, he replies, the Kampuchean people could not overthrow

Pol Pot without Vietnamese help. During his long reign of terror, Pol Pot severely weakened the ability of the Kampuchean people to defend themselves. But the Kampucheans asked for Vietnamese help, he insists, and "it is impossible for a brotherly country to stand aside and watch while brothers are exterminated." Suddenly, the lights go out. I look at my watch; it is 9:30 a.m. One of Mr. Soai's assistants gets up and opens the shutters on the windows, letting in more light.

"Pol Pot tried to solve the class problem in one day," Mr. Soai continues without interruption. "It was a terrible thing." Even through an interpreter, I can sense a degree of earnestness in Mr. Soai's voice, almost a kind of hurt. It is as though he cannot understand why the actions of the Vietnamese have been so misunderstood by the outside world. And indeed, in spite of his occasional lapses into cardboard rhetoric about Marxism-Leninism, the Pol Pot clique and Chinese hegemonism, much of what he is saying squares up with my own knowledge.

I know that Pol Pot's relationship to the Chinese goes back to the days before the Khmer Rouge—the Cambodian communists of Pol Pot—were even a factor in the Indochina war. I know that there is a high correlation between the actions of Pol Pot and the actions of the Chinese in the years since the end of the war, both of which have worked to the detriment of the Vietnamese. I also know, however, that there has been no love lost between Cambodia and Vietnam over the centuries, that many Cambodians feel that much of southern Vietnam including the Saigon region and the Mekong Delta is rightfully Cambodian, not Vietnamese. How much of Pol Pot's actions against the Vietnamese were dictated by an antagonism that, like the Chinese, stands outside the bounds of ideology? But even if that is so, I think, does it help to explain the genocide Pol Pot inflicted on his own country?

Why have Vietnamese forces remained in Kampuchea so long, we ask.

Because the Kampuchean people *want* Vietnamese protection, he insists. "We are ready to withdraw all our forces when Kampuchea requests us to do so, but the Kampucheans are afraid Pol Pot will return."

Why has Thailand offered refuge to Pol Pot and his soldiers?

Because Thailand has territorial interests in Kampuchea, Mr. Soai tells us. Historically, Thailand has invaded Kampuchea and Laos many times. Vietnam has never invaded Thailand, he explains, but in feudal times Thailand invaded Vietnam, and during the U.S. war, Thailand allowed its airfields to be used as bases for American bombing raids against Vietnam.

When will Vietnam withdraw its forces from Kampuchea, we ask.

If a political solution can be found before 1990, he replies, Vietnam will withdraw at the time the solution is found. If no political solution is found by 1990, Vietnam will withdraw anyway because Kampuchea will be strong enough to defend itself by then. "This is not propaganda," he says. "We want to withdraw. Kampuchean cake for Kampucheans only — that is our position."

What conditions are necessary for a political solution, we ask.

Firstly, he replies, it must come in the context of long-term peace and stability in Southeast Asia. Secondly, it must be based on the withdrawal of Vietnamese troops and the elimination of "the Pol Pot clique." "Why should Pol Pot be any part of a negotiated settlement?" he asks. "After World War Two, the fascists were not allowed to participate in the political life of their countries." Finally, he concludes, the Kampuchean people must have self-determination; they must be allowed to settle their own problems.

If the Kampuchean people were to choose a noncommunist government, we ask, would Vietnam be able to accept that?

"So long as Pol Pot is eliminated," Mr. Soai replies, "the Kampucheans can choose their own government. We are not interested in exporting revolution."

"You would really accept a noncommunist Kampuchean government?" John asks a second time.

"So long as Pol Pot is eliminated," Mr. Soai repeats, "the Kampucheans can choose for themselves." I wonder about that one, but there is no point in arguing.

What is Mr. Soai's view of the United States position in all of this, we ask.

United States policy seems undecided, he replies. The United States is not pushing for a negotiated settlement, but it doesn't seem to be willing to close that door entirely. The United States understands the Vietnamese position, he says, but it wants to weaken Vietnam and strengthen its relationship with the Chinese.

Given that the United States has voted every year since 1979 to seat the Pol Pot government in the United Nations General Assembly as the sole legitimate representative of Kampuchea, I am startled by the calmness and evenhandedness of Mr. Soai's analysis of American policy.

General Chi indicates that it is time to go. As we are gathering up our notes, Mr. Soai says, "In the West, people make much of giving humanitarian aid to Kampuchea. Do you know where that aid goes? To Pol Pot's soldiers. If the West wants to give aid to Kampuchea, why don't they give it directly to the Kampuchean people?"

It is almost an anguished outburst, apparently spontaneous and unrehearsed. It is also a charge I have heard before — that Western relief aid is actually being diverted to the remnants of the Khmer Rouge — and there is good reason to believe that it is true. "I don't know," I reply. "People in the West don't understand." I do not tell him that I believe most people in the West don't care to understand.

During lunch, I go for a walk by myself through the stores in downtown Hanoi. I browse through a large bookstore, but there is not a single publication in English and I soon lose interest. I visit an art gallery displaying contemporary oil paintings, and several stores selling lacquer-ware and ivory handicrafts. All of the stores in the downtown area are state-run, and the prices are fixed and nonnegotiable.

High above one intersection is a large poster extolling Lao-Vietnamese friendship: a Lao woman in sarong and a Vietnamese woman in *ao dai* join hands as a white dove hovers over them. On one wall of a nearby building are two more posters: one commemorating the forty-first anniversary of the founding of the army, the other celebrating the unity of workers, soldiers and peasants.

The huge state-run department store sells everything from clothing to cooking utensils to cigarettes. Again, built by the French, it has been here a long time: there are deep depressions in the marble steps leading to the second floor, indicating the passing of many feet. The store seems relatively well-stocked with goods, but the choice of kinds of any given product is limited. In the cigarette department, for instance, the large glass counter display and the glass display shelves behind the counter are all stocked with only one brand of cigarettes. Dozens of cartons — hundreds, even — are stacked in pairs and squares, on end, on their sides, or in pyramids of varying sizes, as though some poor clerk had spent hours trying to find different ways to make this one brand of cigarettes look appealing to the eye.

Everywhere I go, I pass street vendors and tiny stalls selling all kinds of foods. Afraid of contracting diarrhea or worse, I have not bought anything from street vendors except fresh fruit and food that has been served boiling hot. But all week long, I've been tempted by various versions of what we might call a hoagie or hero sandwich. I remember them from the war. We'd been told then, too, not to eat anything that didn't come out of a C-ration carton, but I'd done it anyway, after a few months, and it didn't kill me then. Finally, hunger and nostalgia combine to compel me to give it a try, and I step up to a sidewalk sandwich shop and order one.

I don't have to tell the young woman what I want. From what I can tell, if you want one kind of sandwich, you go to one shop; if you want something else, you go to another shop. On the counter of this shop are loaves of bread — large hoagie-type rolls, really — a huge slab of what appears to be pâté of some sort, and several sticks of meat that look like hard salami or pepperoni. It all looks delicious, actually, but as the woman prepares my sandwich, I find myself wondering what's in the pâté, what's in the sausage, how long has this stuff been sitting out in the open air?

The woman hands me the finished product, wrapped in a piece of stiff newspaper. It must weigh at least two pounds. I hold out a fistful of money, and she giggles and takes several bills. I walk to a nearby park and begin eating. The sandwich is wonderful: the bread thick and chewy with a hard crust, the meat tangy.

Midway through my meal, a small boy of perhaps eight or ten sits down on a bench directly across from me about twenty feet away. He stares at me. I smile and he smiles back. He glances around nervously. Then he gestures furtively, but it is clear what he wants: money. I shake my head no, and continue eating. He glances around again, then gestures as though he were counting bills. Again, I shake my head no. Something is very odd about this exchange, but I can't quite figure out what.

And then it dawns on me: in five days, this is the first incident of begging I've encountered. I think of other places I've been — Hong Kong, Manila, Bangkok, the Bahamas — where armies of cripples and amputees and beggars and children follow one around. Hell, even in Philadelphia, the panhandlers and the bums and the street people are everywhere looking for quarters. Yet here I am in a large city in one of the poorer nations on earth, and I have yet to encounter a beggar until this moment.

And this young fellow is anything but direct in his approach. His eyes dart constantly, and only occasionally does he dare to tender a request. Is it societal condemnation he fears, or merely the police? Whichever it is, it is clear that he is doing something he ought not to be doing, and it is clear that he knows it. He looks like a kid trying to get at the cookie jar.

Giving up on money at last, he changes his approach. He begins rubbing his stomach with the flat of one hand while making exaggerated chewing motions. When that gets no results, he tries to bum a cigarette. Finally, an older man approaches and sits down on a bench next to mine. The boy gives me one last long hard look, then gets up and wanders off.

In the afternoon, we go to the History Museum. General Chi is again absent, and we will not see him until Monday afternoon. As we enter the museum, I can't help noticing a large placard over the doorway carrying a quotation of Ho Chi Minh's. It is in Vietnamese, but I have seen it before and I know what it says: "Nothing is more precious than independence and freedom."

Inside, we begin with a display of bronze drums, some of them quite large. The curator explains that the drums are from a Bronze Age culture centered around the Red River Valley and dating back to 2000 B.C., the earliest beginnings of the Vietnamese as an identifiable group. The drums, she says, are believed by archeologists to be indigenous to Vietnam, though some have been found in southern China, Thailand and Malaysia, and even as far away as Sumatra and Java. Similar drums can be found still in use by the Muong tribes, whom the curator explains come from the same cultural and ethnic ancestry as the Vietnamese, the two groups not diverging until around a thousand years ago. There are other displays of Bronze Age artifacts, along with several human skeletons. "Birds have nests," the curator says as we stand looking at one of the skeletons lying in the remains of a dugout canoe that must have served as a coffin, "men have ancestors."

After the Bronze Age displays come a series of exhibits and dioramas depicting the many battles of the Vietnamese against foreign invaders. The curator calls the Battle of Bach Dang River, in A.D. 938, a "Chinese Dien Bien Phu." It is the battle which finally broke the hold of China over the Vietnamese after a thousand years of Chinese occupation. She explains that the Vietnamese defeated the Chinese by placing sharpened tree trunks in the riverbed to impede the movements of the large Chinese ships, meanwhile leaving themselves free to maneuver at will with their smaller boats. The tactics strike me as being remarkably similar to those often used against the Americans over a thousand years later.

Other displays depict the defeat of Chinese invasions in 981 and 1076–77, Mongol invasions in 1215, 1285 and 1288, still more Chinese invasions, then an invasion of the Mekong Delta region by the Thais in 1784–85. Finally, there is another Chinese invasion repulsed at the gates of Hanoi in 1789 by a surprise attack during Tet. This, too, carries echoes of more recent history.

Above one of the battle dioramas is a large plaque with an inscription. I ask Loan what it says. "Oh, that is a very famous poem," she replies. It was written by General Ly Thuong Kiet on the eve of a great victory over the Chinese in 1077:

> Over the mountains and rivers of Vietnam reigns the Emperor
>   of Vietnam,
> As it stands written in the Book of Heaven.
> How is it that you strangers dare to invade our land?
> Your armies, without pity, shall be annihilated.

When Loan has finished reciting, the curator tells us that Vietnamese negotiator Le Duc Tho once recited this poem to Henry Kissinger during the Paris Peace Talks.

Mrs. Troan and Mr. Hoang call it a day once we are finished at the museum, but Loan asks us if we want to visit Dong Xuan Market in Old Hanoi. The market is crowded and bustling, and Loan quietly warns us to be careful of pickpockets. Unlike the state-run stores downtown, there is much haggling over prices and the variety of goods is much greater: there is almost everything imaginable from pineapples to antique buddhas. Loan explains that these essentially private enterprises must pay a tax to the state. I buy a small carved wooden water buffalo for myself, then buy a pair of delicate silver earrings for Anne.

"Don't get mixed up between old dong and new dong," Loan says, checking to see that I have not paid too much for the earrings. Our visit to Vietnam happens to come at a time when the entire monetary system is being converted: ten old dong are worth one new dong, but both old and new dong are still in circulation. The bills aren't that different from each other, and it is easy for an outsider like me to get confused. If you get it wrong, you end up paying ten times the actual purchase price — though so far, shopkeepers and vendors have been very tolerant (and honest), correcting my mistakes for me.

When Loan wanders off to check on Bruce and John, the man at the jewelry stall asks me if I want to change dollars for dong. I ask how much. One hundred dong to the dollar, he replies — over seven times the official exchange rate and twice what the hotel night clerk had offered me a few days earlier. I find myself tempted. *Am* I being watched, I wonder. I decide that the last thing I need is trouble with the authorities. Things aren't that expensive anyway, I tell myself as I leave, not quite convinced.

Out in the street a trolley is passing by. The trolleys of Hanoi are —
well — quaint. There's no other word for it. Yet another legacy of the
French, they are powered by electricity and run on narrow-gauge rails set
flush with the street surface. The cars, most of them painted bright
yellow, have permanently open windows with no glass, and there are no
doors. Inching along slowly, groaning and creaking, they look like relics
from the 1920s, which is probably exactly what they are. Certainly, none
of the cars is newer than the end of the French Indochina War. As this
one passes, two small boys jump onto the rear coupling, hitching a free
ride and obviously delighted with themselves.

After a supper of *bun cha*, a dish similar to *pho*, we are walking back
toward the hotel when we suddenly come upon a Catholic cathedral.
Loan asks if we want to go in. Inside, perhaps 150 people are sitting in
the pews. There is no priest, but people seem to be chanting the rosary.
Loan says that mass will be said later in the evening, explaining that in
many churches like this one, services are still held. In one corner of the
church is a decorated Christmas tree and a manger scene. All of the
human figures around the manger are Caucasian.

As we talk quietly, an old woman walks up to Loan and begins scold-
ing her about something. Loan tries to ignore her, but the old woman
refuses to be put off. Instead, she becomes even more vocal and begins
to gesticulate wildly. Other people are beginning to turn in their seats,
staring, trying to see what the commotion is all about. The old woman
continues to shout at Loan, her gestures indicating that she wants Loan
to leave immediately. Loan is clearly embarrassed and flustered. I think
she is about to begin crying. "Let's get out of here," I say, "We've seen
enough, anyway."

Loan doesn't reply, but doesn't resist when I take her by the arm and
lead her out into the night air. The old woman follows us all the way to
the door, hurling what can only be a few choice epithets after us. What
was that all about, we ask. Loan just shakes her head. She is pale, visibly
shaken, her eyes full of tears. Did the old woman think we were
heathens? Russians? Americans? Did she think Loan was a prostitute and
we her clients? Was she just plain crazy? What *was* that all about? But
Loan will not tell us. "We must walk quickly," she says finally. "We'll be
late for the theatre."

Nha Hat Lon, the Big Theatre, was built in 1911. Loan tells us it is
an exact replica of a theatre in Paris, producing four tickets from her
pocket as she does so. I wonder when she bought them. We try to repay
her, but she won't let us. Inside, it is dimly lit and filling up quickly as

we find our seats in the second-floor balcony. The audience seems to consist entirely of young people in their teens and twenties. Here and there, couples sit together, some shyly holding hands in the semidarkness. It reminds me of going to the movies in the years before I was old enough to drive and bold enough to want something more than holding hands.

The performance tonight is a kind of variety show put on by the Youth Ensemble. Most of the show consists of what I take to be popular songs performed by various groups that include — in different combinations — vocalists, guitars, drums, violins, trumpets and saxaphones. It strikes me as an Asian throwback to American and British pop-rock of the early 1960s: members of each band wear color-coordinated stylized clothes, trios of back-up singers all dressed alike move in well-rehearsed unison to the music, stage lighting changes unimaginatively from blue to red to yellow, and the music itself seems painfully obsolete.

Knowing that socialist countries generally frown on contemporary Western rock-and-roll as one of the most decadent elements of the capitalist world, I wonder if what I'm seeing is what the performers would like to be doing — or is it only as wild and crazy as the state will allow them to get? The audience certainly doesn't seem to be terribly impressed. The applause between each number is, to my sensibilities, so minimal as to be almost insulting. Or is this the usual audience response in Vietnam? Having come of age listening to Jimi Hendrix mangle the Star-Spangled Banner while practically masturbating with his guitar as the audience danced in the aisles and screamed bloody murder, I have absolutely no yardstick by which to judge either the performers or the audience.

Occasionally, a single female vocalist dressed in an *ao dai* comes out and sings what seems to be a more traditional Vietnamese song. And two mimes perform a wonderful skit about making a new suit of clothing, the humor of which requires no translation. The routine brings the house down, making previous audience response all the more suspect.

One routine, however, is very different from anything else. As a single female vocalist begins to sing somewhere offstage, a man dressed as a peasant appears in the circle of a spotlight at the center of a bare stage. He is holding a flat basket — the only prop he will use throughout the routine — and though the basket is empty, his gestures clearly indicate that the basket holds an infant. The man rocks the basket rhythmically as the voice offstage sings a gentle lullabye. Then he places the baby on the ground and begins to plant rice, rapidly taking the shoots from the basket, one slim shoot at a time. So skillful is this mime that the ricefield in which he works appears in the mind's eye so clearly I can smell the water, feel the cool mud sucking at my feet, see the new green shoots as his deft hands shove them down into the mud.

But then a siren begins to sound, its wail rising to a steady scream. Alarmed, the farmer takes up his child and hides him in a shelter as the back of the stage begins to flash yellow and red, guns begin to boom, and bombs begin to whistle and explode. We hear the baby's frightened crying, see the father's efforts to comfort his child.

Finally, in frustration, the father climbs out of the shelter. Using the basket for a helmet, he takes up a rifle and begins firing up at the sky. He is wounded. He staggers, falls, gets up, and staggers again. Crawling to his infant's side, he rises on one knee and cradles the child to his breast, then places it gently in the basket. The sounds of battle have passed now. The lullabye begins again. Bending his head low, the farmer kisses his child once on the forehead, then slowly sinks to the ground. Again, the child begins to cry. The spotlight narrows down to a single small circle of white light resting on the empty straw basket.

Sunday, December 22

The Children's Palace is a kind of school for extracurricular activities. Children between the ages of 4 and 15 come here after the regular school day is over, and on weekends. It offers training in music, dance, painting, film, drama, various sports, and a variety of technical and vocational subjects. As we sip tea, the director explains that the school was founded in 1955, and that 3.8 million children have attended since then. Currently, 200 teachers handle 4,500 children each week. The director is very proud of the fact that Jane Fonda has visited the school and Pete Seeger once performed here.

How is one chosen to attend the school, we ask. Every child in Hanoi is eligible, he responds. I think of the beggar boy in the park yesterday, of the dozens of children I've seen playing in the gutters of the alleys of Old Hanoi. Are they eligible, too, I wonder.

Before we tour the school, we must visit the school's museum. We are met at the door by a stern-looking, thin, middle-aged woman with a lecturer's pointer in hand. She begins with an exhibit I call "Uncle Ho and the Children." With funereal solemnity, the woman explains how much Ho Chi Minh loved children. All children. To prove this, she points to a wall of photographs. Stopping before each one, she extends her pointer crisply and tells us:

"This is Uncle Ho with the children of the south."
"This is Uncle Ho with the children of the north."
"This is Uncle Ho with the children of the minorities."
"This is Uncle Ho with the children of Hungary."
"This is Uncle Ho with the children of Czechoslovakia."
"This is Uncle Ho with the children of Moscow."

In between each explanation, she pauses for a minute or two to allow the full import of what she is saying to sink in. Long before she has finished with one wall of one room in an exhibition in which I can see at

73

least three more rooms, I am acutely aware that this is going to be a very long morning. Of all the people I have met thus far, this woman strikes me as the spitting image of my notion of a true hard-core Party cadre. She has no sense of humor. She doesn't know how to smile. She wields her pointer like a colonel giving a briefing at the Pentagon. I cannot imagine a worse person to be found in the presence of children. I can imagine her in a small room with a single naked lightbulb, blackjack in hand, interrogating a suspected murderer. I am certain she would always get a confession. I wish dearly that I hadn't bothered getting up this morning.

An hour later, she is still at it. Here is a portrait of one of the school's most famous graduates, she explains. Here are the medals he won in the war for shooting down Yankee imperialist aggressor airplanes. Here are the drawings of younger students depicting this hero shooting down the airplanes of the Yankee imperialist aggressors. Hey, lady, I want to tell her, I wasn't exactly a big fan of the war, but those are my countrymen going down in flames there. She has the sensitivity of a Mack truck. I am ready to confess. I wonder if I can feign illness and walk back to the hotel.

Though I have begun to despair that the moment would ever come, at last we have seen every photograph, drawing, ribbon, medal, trophy, handicraft and artifact ever invented, awarded or created, and we leave the Commissar and her House of Horrors behind. My head aches. We enter another building and the director ushers us into a small elevator. It is a tight fit. The building has only three stories, and we get off on the second floor. It's the first elevator I've encountered in Hanoi, and it occurs to me that the director is eager to demonstrate that it works.

We visit several classrooms where elementary-age children are painting watercolors and working with modeling clay. Then we enter a small ballet practice room with mirrors and a waist-high railing along two walls. Chairs are arranged in two rows at one end of the room, and as the director seats us, he explains that some of the children have prepared a special show for us this morning. Along one wall, a door to a dressing room is partially open, and I can see several girls in ill-fitting leotards peeking out. They look nervous.

For the next hour, we are treated to a variety of songs and dances by performers ranging from perhaps 8 to 13. And it really is a treat. One young girl performs a kind of dance using hoops that look and work like Hula Hoops except that she manages to get about 15 of them going all at once. Then a group of eight girls performs what we are told is a traditional minority dance. Then a small chorus sings several songs. Throughout the performance, a small combo consisting of boys playing an accordion, a trumpet, a saxophone and a clarinet provides the accompaniment. The kids are obviously having a fine time strutting their stuff. It reminds me of parents day at the local elementary school; there is that same combination of unsophisticated nervousness and sheer exuberance that is genuinely ice-melting. I am glad now that I didn't beg off in the middle of the Ice Lady's Re-education Camp.

Finally, an older girl of perhaps 15 takes the floor alone and sings, in English and without accompaniment, "We Shall Overcome." Her diction is perfect, her delivery confident. It is clearly for our benefit—sheer propaganda, one might even say—but it is effective and very moving. When she finishes, all of the other children swarm around her and hug her and hug each other, and then the band begins again and the children rush over to us and physically drag us onto the floor and there we all are—Mrs. Troan and Mr. Hoang and Loan and the two drivers and John and Bruce and I and the director and all the munchkins—joining hands in a simple, energetic circle dance, whirling and skip-stepping and working up a good sweat. I haven't had so much fun in days, in weeks. The kids laugh and watch our faces, looking for approval, and I laugh and hold their hands firmly, and I wish it could always be this simple, and it makes me sad because I know it never will be.

The afternoon and evening are ours, Loan explains later as we ride back to the hotel. She and the others will meet us Monday morning at eight. What will she do with the rest of the day, we ask. She giggles, covers her mouth quickly with her hand, and explains that she is going to visit "friends."

"You've got a boyfriend, don't you?" I say.

"Want to borrow some of my Gecko Elixir?" John teases. Loan blushes and laughs, waving us out of the car with an air of exaggerated impatience.

Setting off on foot toward Old Hanoi, John, Bruce and I decide to go exploring. I want to take a closer look at Long Bien Bridge, the railroad bridge spanning the Red River. From a distance, its superstructure is jagged and unsymmetrical, as though it had been bombed and repaired many times, as undoubtedly it had been during the war. People are everywhere as we walk. Sunday is the one day most Vietnamese have off, and today is pleasantly warm and almost sunny. At the base of the bridge, a large bus depot bustles with people and buses coming and going. Beyond the depot rises the massive earthen dike that protects Hanoi from the floodwaters of the Red River.

We climb to the top of the dike only to discover that the river itself is still several hundred meters away. On top of the dike is an unpaved roadway wide enough for two cars to pass, though the only traffic is pedestrians and bicycles, an occasional ox-cart or motorscooter. Between the dike and the river is a broad plain speckled with fields of vegetable gardens separated by small dikes, and houses standing alone or in small groups, each surrounded by tall trees and plants to provide privacy. Here and there, men and women are tending the fields, bare-footed, dressed in the loose pajama-like clothes typical of working peasants.

One woman carries two large square cans of water attached to either end of a stout pole resting across her shoulders at the base of her neck. As she walks among the rows of cabbage plants, she waters the plants by tipping the cans forward until the water spills out through tiny holes forming makeshift sprinklers. When the cans are empty, she trots back to the well, refills the cans, and repeats the process. Endlessly. Patiently. It is hard to believe this lush rural village environment exists barely thirty minutes' walk from the hotel. But it must also be a precarious existence: the fields and houses lie between the riverbank and the flood dikes; whenever the river rises enough to threaten the city, it must inevitably leave these homes and fields under water.

As we step along the small dikes between fields, for the first time I find myself uneasy, nervous in a way I cannot quite explain. There is nothing to fear, I know, but this place is so much like the hamlets and fields I once patrolled day in and day out: tripwires, punji pits, mines and boobytraps, hedgerows suddenly erupting with gunfire, hot bloody death without warning. It isn't as though I'm about to freak out, or anything like that. It's just a feeling. A vague discomfort: you've been here before—watch your step. Bruce feels it, too. Adrenalin fear so deeply imbedded that even the passage of 18 years cannot quite erase it.

A train starts across the bridge several hundred meters to our right. The cars—an odd assortment of shapes and colors, the passengers visible through the open windows—are pulled by a small steam locomotive. I haven't seen a working steam locomotive in years. I wave to the engineer, and he waves back.

We continue on to the riverbank only to discover that the water level is still 30 to 40 feet below us. The bank here has been shaped and chan-neled by an artificial stone wall that slopes away from us at a 45-degree angle down to the water. Perhaps as much as a mile wide, the river is low this time of year, and we can see exposed sand flats and broad shoals between us and the opposite bank. Directly below us, half a dozen men are gathered at the stern of a motorized barge moored to the bank. The men seem to be smoking something: tobacco, marijuana, opium? They wave up at us, smiling, and vigorously gesture for us to join them. We wave back, but decline their offer.

Finally, we head back into the city, deciding to follow a course roughly parallel to the south bank of the river, which will take us through a part of the city we haven't seen before. Yesterday, I'd noticed that the History Museum is located near the river dike. We should come to the museum eventually, and from there I know my way back to the hotel.

As we walk, whole families ride by on a single bicycle: the man pedaling, the woman behind with an infant in arms, another small child perched on the handlebars. Lovers take the opportunity to ride double, allowing the woman to put her arms around the man's waist, a kind of public physical contact between men and women that is otherwise frowned upon by society. Periodically, creaking yellow trolleys slowly clank by. On every street corner, a bicycle repairman waits for customers, squatting on the curb smoking, his patching kit stuffed in an old green ammunition box, bicycle pump in hand. We buy balls of sweet fried dough that resemble drop-donuts from a street vendor. She lifts them directly from the sizzling oil with a pair of chopsticks and plops them onto small squares of old newsprint that take the place of napkins.

But the History Museum doesn't seem to be where I thought it would be. We've been walking for over an hour since we left the railroad bridge, and I finally have to admit to Bruce and John that I'm lost. "Some scout you must have been," Bruce teases. John asks a policeman for directions and we take off at right angles to our present line of travel. The crush of pedestrians and bicycles is increasing. Afternoon is wearing on, and people seem to be heading home now.

After more than another hour, however, we are still not finding anything that looks familiar. We are all getting more than a little sore of foot, and it is getting dark, and the temperature is dropping. Suddenly I recognize the park that surrounds Van Mieu Pagoda, which does us no good at all because none of us can remember how we got from the hotel to the pagoda. John asks another policeman for directions. The policeman deliberates with a cyclo driver and a young woman on a bicycle. For several minutes, they cannot seem to come to an agreement about which way we should go, but at last they seem satisfied with their conclusion. They point us down a wide boulevard and indicate that we should turn left when it dead-ends.

This boulevard looks familiar, we realize. There are a number of foreign embassies on this street, and we've passed by here before. But we can't remember when, or where we were coming from, or where we were going to. We finally reach the end of the street, turn left and keep walking, passing by a larger-than-life-sized statue of Lenin. I've seen that statue before — on the morning we visited Ho Chi Minh's mausoleum. And sure enough, further on, we come to the edge of the huge square across from the mausoleum. But none of us can remember how we got from the hotel to the mausoleum. It is nearly dark now, the sun setting in a brilliant red sky behind the mausoleum, and it has begun to drizzle.

Cold and dog-tired from five hours of walking, we finally conclude that there is nothing for it but to hire a cyclo to get us back. It takes another 45 minutes to locate one. We settle on a price — 50 dong — and all three of us climb aboard, which is no easy task: Bruce sits in the seat while John and I sit on either arm. It is now pitch dark. As the driver peddles along, working very hard to propel his 450-pound load, John tries to talk to him, but about all we can discover is that he likes "Hotel California," a song by the Eagles, an American rock band.

After awhile, I begin to suspect that we are not going in the right direction. We seem to be headed out of the city, rather than into it, but my directional credibility with John and Bruce has long since evaporated, and they tell me rudely and gaily to shut the hell up. Perched precariously on the narrow wicker arm of the cyclo chair, my rear end and left leg are asleep, which sounds more benign than it feels.

Suddenly, Bruce smacks John and me, points up ahead and says, "Bill was right." Only a few hundred yards up is the Thang Long Hotel, where we had dinner with Mrs. Thuc and Mr. Hung. The Thang Long Hotel is on the edge of the city, a very long way from the Thong Nhat. There is much shouting and general pandemonium. John begins to talk to the driver, and I can't understand anything he's saying except the words "Thang Long."

"What hotel are you asking for, John?" I interrupt.

"The Thang Long."

"That's the Thang Long," I reply, pointing, "We're staying at the Thong Nhat."

"Oops," says John.

"Nice work," says Bruce.

"You wanna try explaining this one to the driver?" I tell John.

"No," says John.

But he does. And it isn't what the driver wants to hear. He is panting hard and drenched in sweat. At first he refuses to budge, as if he can't believe what John is saying. Then he asks for more money—double the price we'd agreed on. We have no choice but to agree. He shakes his head, as if to say, "These Americans are crazy," then turns around and off we go again.

At one point we are stopped by a policeman. There is a brief conversation between the cyclo driver and the cop, and then we are off again. What was that about, we ask John.

"I think it's illegal to ride three to a cyclo," John replies, "But the guy explained that we're Americans and we're lost, and the cop told him to beat it."

Our driver is pedalling furiously now. On one narrow street, we overtake a trolley car. Bruce, John and I are cheering and urging our driver on, the trolley passengers are hanging out the windows and laughing and pointing, and when we finally draw up even with the trolley driver, he waves and smiles and rings the trolley's bell. And then we are cruising around the far side of Restoration Sword Lake, and there's Indira Gandhi Park, and the Central Bank building, and the ministry building, and finally the hotel.

Our driver is whipped. He leans heavily over the handlebars, breathing like he's just gone 15 rounds with Joe Frazier, then looks up and grins. "Nice work," we tell him. "Number One." We decide to pay him 150 dong—50 apiece—half again as much as he'd asked for and probably as much as he'd normally make in a month. Bruce throws in a pack of "555" English cigarettes. I am so stiff, I can hardly walk. Inside the hotel, we discover a decorated Christmas tree standing in the lobby. The restaurant has been closed for hours. I am too tired to eat anyway.

Monday, December 23

At the Writers' Union, we are received by Phan Cu De, professor of literature at Hanoi University, and Vuong Trong, an army captain and an active poet. Captain Trong is especially interested in poems written by American veterans of the war. He is very pleased when we offer him a copy of my anthology, *Carrying the Darkness*, published only a few months earlier. When I point out that it also contains poems by Bruce and John, he asks all three of us to sign the book for him. He explains that he graduated from Hanoi University in 1965 with a degree in mathematics, that he has been in the army ever since, but that his first love has always been poetry.

It is not so unusual to find a mathematician and army captain who also writes and publishes poetry. Poetry is an active part of day-to-day life and culture in Vietnam. Ho Chi Minh was a poet, and a good one. To Huu, a current member of the Vietnamese ruling politburo, is also one of Vietnam's two most highly-regarded living poets. General Chi, Mrs. Troan and even young Loan have found frequent occasions to recite poems for us; all seem to know dozens — perhaps hundreds — of poems by heart, and take great pleasure in the music of ordered language. From the *ca dao* of peasant farmers to the Poet's Balcony at Van Mieu Pagoda to the daily newspapers, poetry is everywhere in Vietnam. It leaves American poets like us fairly drooling with envy.

Still, in Vietnam today, poetry — like virtually everything else — is a function of the state, if not the actual writing, at least its publication, and I do not envy that. How does one become a member of the Writers' Union, we ask. A poet must already have published poems, Professor De explains, and he or she must be sponsored by two current members of the Union. And how does one get poems published, we ask. By submitting them to magazines and newspapers, we are told.

What about censorship, we ask. The professor doesn't seem to understand the question. What if a poet writes a poem critical of the government or of present conditions in Vietnam, we explain; can a poem like that get published? The answer we receive is oblique and confusing, and additional questions bring no further illumination. Again, I find myself wondering if the problem is merely Loan's lack of translating skills. I cannot help noticing what seems to be a curious pattern: over the past week, each time we've asked what might be called a "sensitive" question, our translators' skills seem to break down, and we always end up with nonanswers. It seems that in Vietnam today, certain topics, certain aspects of history, certain facts of contemporary life are simply beyond discussion.

I didn't have to come here, of course, to discover that; I already knew that Vietnam is not an open society. Still, the constant reminders are sometimes disconcerting. What would happen to a person like me in Vietnam today—a constant and vocal critic of my government and its policies? Re-education, perhaps? Prison? I have to remind myself that I would doubtless fare no better in countries like Guatemala, South Korea or Pakistan—all allies and clients of the United States, part of what my government still insists upon calling the "Free World."

As we are talking over tea and tangerines, a much older man suddenly rushes in looking harried and out of breath. He apologizes for being late and introduces himself as Te Hanh. I recognize the name immediately; I have read his poetry. Along with To Huu, Te Hanh is the other most revered living Vietnamese poet. This, indeed, is a great honor—the Vietnamese equivalent of an audience with Robert Penn Warren or Robert Bly. General Chi and his staff must have decided that we really are okay.

We offer our condolences at the recent death of Xuan Dieu, another contemporary Vietnamese poet. Te Hanh runs his fingers through his thinning gray hair and peers at us for a moment with keen eyes. He seems a little surprised that we know of his colleague, and genuinely moved that we have taken the trouble to note his passing.

"We were friends for a very long time," he says at last, his eyes misting. Then he picks up the translated copy of "Making the Children Behave," which has been lying on the table. "Which of you wrote this?" he asks.

"I did," I reply.

Excitedly, he reaches for a fat English-language anthology called *Vietnamese Literature* and begins to flip through it until he locates what he is looking for. Smiling, he hands the book to me and points to the open page. "Read this," he says. It is a poem of his called "Questions Underground":

When there are no more bombs to the children of the South,
shall I be let to go on the earth again?
Why do you ask, little one...
I want to see the sky, Mother, are the clouds blue?
I want to see the sun, is the light really golden?

When there are no more bombs,
shall I be let to go on the earth again?
Why do you ask, little one...
I want to see the trees, are the leaves living yet?
I want to see the flowers, do they smell sweet, Mama?

When there are no more bombs,
shall I be let to go up on the earth again?
Why do you ask, little one...
I want to see the road, where does it go, Mama?
I want to see our village,
are there still rice-fields and gardens, Mama?

When there are no more bombs,
shall you let me go up on the earth again?
Why do you keep asking, little one...
I want to see the uncles and aunts I loved,
are they still fighting, Mama?
I want to see the Yankee,
Mama, does it look like a human being?

On our way back to the hotel, we stop by the Ambassadors' Pagoda. Loan tells us that it got its name because in ancient times foreign ambassadors to Vietnam sent their children here to be educated. It is still an active pagoda, she explains, and indeed, in many of the side rooms, young robed monks with shaven heads appear to be studying old texts. In the main temple, Loan bows respectfully to the old monk in attendance, takes three sticks of incense, lights them, and plants them in a large earth-filled urn in front of a statue of the Buddha. She stands before the Buddha for several minutes, head bowed as if in prayer. Is she praying — or is this simply for our benefit? But the question seems too rude, and I do not ask it. Though I have not prayed to a Christian God in two decades, I had found myself praying to Buddha in front of the hotel in Bangkok only nine days earlier. And I had meant it. It is always a dangerous thing to impugn the motives of others.

In the afternoon, we return to the ministry building for a final session with General Chi before we leave Hanoi. It soon becomes apparent that the afternoon is an extended plea for better relations between Vietnam and the United States. "Our two countries have a bitter history," he begins, "but that does not have to be an obstacle to better relations in the future." As has so often been the case with those with whom we've talked over the course of the previous week, the general turns to Vietnamese history to make his point.

In the 13th century, he says, when Chinese invaders realized they couldn't defeat Vietnam, the Vietnamese were willing to make peace in a way that allowed the Chinese to save face. The same thing happened again in the 15th century, the Vietnamese initiating a truce in order to allow the Chinese an honorable withdrawal. In the 18th century, the Vietnamese even provided invading Chinese troops with boots and horses in order to facilitate their withdrawal. And even after nearly a century of French colonial rule and a bitter eight-year war, Vietnam and France have since enjoyed good relations. "We want normal relations with the U.S.," General Chi says, "We would like to forget the unhappy past."

He tells us that Vietnam is willing to normalize relations without any preconditions. It is the United States, he says, that insists upon preconditions, specifically resolution of the MIA problem and the question of Amerasian children. The United States insists that all Americans missing in action must be accounted for, and claims that Vietnam has not been cooperative. But the Vietnamese, he says, have demonstrated "good will" repeatedly, turning over nearly 100 sets of remains since the end of the war and allowing American excavation teams to come to Vietnam to search for MIAs. He cites one example of a joint U.S.-Vietnamese search team that even had to destroy several houses in order to excavate a crash site. All that was found were part of an aircraft wing, a helmet and a few bone fragments; so little remained that American technical personnel couldn't even determine whether or not the bone chips belonged to a U.S. pilot. And for this, he says, several Vietnamese families lost their homes. "We are doing all that we can to help locate and return American remains," he says, "but the U.S. administration has distorted our good intentions."

As for Amerasian children, he says, the Vietnamese have long been willing to repatriate all Amerasian children who wish to leave, but the United States has imposed many complicated conditions for acceptance of these children. They are treated just like any other refugees by the United States, rather than being given the special status they deserve by virtue of their parentage. He points out that, by U.S. law, since these children have American fathers, they are already American citizens and ought to be recognized and accepted as such. Instead, they must provide answers to over 100 questions before they can be approved for repatriation; many of these questions, such as the exact identity of the father, simply cannot be answered, thus eliminating any possibility of repatriation.

What about Kampuchea, I ask. Hasn't the United States insisted upon Vietnamese withdrawal from Kampuchea as a condition for normalization? Yes, he replies, but again he argues that it is not up to the Vietnamese. What has happened in Kampuchea is the responsibility of the Chinese; it is part of a long-term Chinese plan to weaken Vietnam. He argues that China urged Pol Pot to attack Vietnam in late 1978, that when Vietnamese forces overwhelmed Pol Pot much more easily than the Chinese expected, China mobilized 600,000 troops along the northern border in February 1979 to try to divert regular Vietnamese army troops from Kampuchea in order to save Pol Pot. The plan didn't work, he says, because local Vietnamese militia units were able to turn back the Chinese invasion without the assistance of regulars.

As proof that China has long actively tried to undermine Vietnamese independence, he points out that the Chinese pressured Ho Chi Minh to accept the temporary partition of Vietnam in 1954. Chinese aid to north Vietnam in later years was always enough to keep the war going, but never enough to be decisive. "China has always been willing to fight to the last Vietnamese," he says, chuckling softly. Moreover, in late 1974 and early 1975, China actually offered to send money and military assistance to the "puppet regime" of Nguyen Van Thieu in order to prolong the war and thwart the victory of the revolutionary forces.

This last assertion is real news to me — something I have never heard before. "Are you sure about this?" I ask. Yes, he insists, and he suggests that Gerald Ford and Henry Kissinger were aware of it and may even have encouraged it.

The notion is intriguing. Certainly, after 1972, U.S.-Chinese relations improved steadily. And by late 1974, the Ford-Kissinger administration was finding it increasingly more difficult to channel additional funds to the Thieu regime in the face of widespread congressional and public opposition to continued aid. And undoubtedly, given the historical fact of Chinese fear of a unified and strong Vietnam, China might well have seen advantages to keeping the Thieu regime afloat. Stranger marriages have occurred in the world of international politics.

"So you see," General Chi concludes, "normalization does not depend completely on us. We think normalization will profit both sides, and we regret that the U.S. administration does not have the same priorities that we do." Still, he says, the failure to achieve normalization will not prevent the Vietnamese from going forward. "We face many difficulties," he says, "but we are a patient people."

Near the end of his talk, he is joined by another man we have not met before. He is introduced as Mr. Chinh, a member of the Vietnamese parliament and president of the War Crimes Commission. Mr. Chinh apologizes for not having met with us earlier in the week, explaining that parliament has been in session, requiring his attendance. He invites us to join him and General Chi for dinner.

Accompanied only by Loan, who will serve as translator, the five of us get into Mr. Chinh's car, a black Russian Volga sedan, and drive across town to a restaurant that reminds me vaguely of a Vietnamese version of a German beer hall. The interior is one large room with a concrete floor packed tightly with folding tables and chairs. The woman in charge seems to know Chinh and Chi, and escorts us quickly to a table. Two helpers set up a portable partition made of cloth stretched over a wooden frame that affords us some privacy from the rest of the customers, perhaps in deference to the rank of our hosts. The meal consists of eel soup, boiled turtle, shrimp, crabs, frogs' legs, pork, rice, salad and beer, along with a bottle of *lua moi* rice vodka.

As we eat, we learn that Mr. Chinh is also a former soldier. "Everyone is a veteran," he says, "or almost everyone. We were made soldiers by the French colonialists, the Japanese fascists, the American imperialists, and now the Chinese expansionists. We love peace very much, but wanting peace and having it are not the same thing. We will always be ready to defend our homeland." General Chinh explains that he started out as a guerrilla fighter against the Japanese during World War Two. Later, he was captured by the French, but managed to escape. Eventually, he rose to the rank of four-star general, but like General Chi, he has other duties to perform these days.

General Chi mentions to General Chinh that I had once been stationed at Con Thien, a much besieged Marine outpost up on the

Demilitarized Zone. When was I there, General Chinh asks. November
and December 1967, I reply. He smiles and nods, explaining that during
that time he commanded a headquarters unit engaged against Con
Thien. What did he think of us, I ask.

"You held your ground," he replies, smiling again.

"That's about all we held," I reply, laughing. "Every time we
stepped outside the perimeter wire, we got our backsides kicked. You
knew everything we were doing, didn't you?"

General Chinh laughs, his head lifting easily and his mouth opening. His teeth — what is left of them — look awful. So do General Chi's —
the result, no doubt, of years in the field without dental care of any
kind.

"We weren't very effective, were we?" I say.

"You were — brave," he replies.

"You are too diplomatic," I respond, "General Chi won't answer
that question, either" — at this, General Chi begins to laugh — "Seriously, what did you think of us?"

"Your fixed positions were useless," General Chinh replies, "You
were too dependent on your helicopters and air support. You did not
know how to become one with the land, and so you sacrificed true mo-
bility for a false sense of security."

"Would it have mattered if we had done things differently?"
I ask.

"No," he replies after a pause, "Probably not. History was not on
your side. We were fighting for our homeland. What were you fighting
for?"

For a long moment, I think of Lyndon Johnson and the beaches of
Waikiki, the miserable corruption of successive Saigon regimes, the
pride and vanity of men like Walt Rostow and Robert McNamara and
Henry Kissinger, and Richard Nixon's shrill insistence on "peace with
honor." I think of my own enlistment at age 17, the inflexible certainty
of my decision, and the terrible collective ignorance of the small town
that buried half a dozen of my high school classmates.

"Nothing that really mattered," I reply.

General Chi reaches for the bottle of *lua moi* and refills everyone's
glass. "We must not forget the past," he says, "but we must live for the
future." The two old generals salute us with their glasses, then turn to
each other and drink. Their eyes shine brightly. They dote on us like
kindly grandfathers, urging us to eat, passing the frog's legs and the turtle meat still another time. Between the two of them, they represent six

general's stars and 85 years of revolutionary struggle, war, sacrifice and hardship. I can only imagine what they have endured, how many of their comrades they left behind in the jungles. But they were always certain of what they were fighting for, and whatever else they may or may not be, they are winners.

Ho Chi Minh City

Though it is still dark at 5:45 a.m. as we head into the countryside toward the airport, already the roads are beginning to stir with the first people moving toward the city: factory workers, farmers with bicycles loaded with fresh produce, students. As dawn approaches, we pass several low-walled, neatly cared-for cemeteries decorated with banners in the national colors of red and yellow. Loan explains that these are "heroes' cemeteries," the graves of soldiers killed defending the homeland.

General Chi, Mrs. Troan and Mr. Hoang are waiting at the terminal when we arrive. The general introduces us to his wife, a short stout woman who has come to see him off. She is a native southerner, he explains. She asks about our wives and families, smiling and nodding as John and Bruce show her photographs of their children. She asks if I have any children yet. When I tell her, "Not yet, but my wife and I are practicing very hard," she laughs with approval. "We have seven children," she says, "but that required many years of practice."

When our flight is called, we say goodbye to Mrs. Troan, Mr. Hoang and Miss Loan. It is an awkward moment. I have come to feel comfortable with these people, and I know that I will probably never see any of them again. I wonder for a moment if it would be proper to give the women a kiss, then decide, oh, what the hell, and give Mrs. Troan and Loan each a hug and a kiss. They both seem startled, and pleased. "Live long and be happy," I whisper in Loan's ear, and she squeezes my hand tightly before letting it go.

Uniformed officers check our passports and visas as we leave the terminal, then we walk across the tarmac to the waiting four-engine Russian-built turboprop. The flight is very full, and we are unable to find four seats together, so I take an open seat alone by a window. Soon after we reach altitude, stewardesses serve the most remarkable breakfast I have ever encountered, in-flight or anywhere else: tea, a banana, a sweet candy-like bean cake, two sesame seed candy sticks, several pieces of molasses taffy, and an entire packet of sugar cookies like the ones we were served at the orphanage school. Though I have a fondness for sweet things, it is a bit much at 8:30 in the morning, and I leave most of it uneaten.

The flight, which cost $150 payable in dollars, will take two and a half hours. Halfway into the flight, I realize that we must be passing over central Vietnam right about now. Somewhere below me are Con Thien, Hue, Danang and Hoi An. This is as close as I will ever get to the places so deeply etched into my memory so long ago. Once again, a terrible wave of disappointment washes over me, and I strain for a glimpse of the ground below, turning and twisting in my seat, but there is nothing to see except an unbroken expanse of thick clouds.

Does it really matter, I wonder, feeling a little ashamed of myself. After all, here is a poor nation struggling to cope with enormous difficulties, and I have been pouting all week long because I haven't been able to act out my own private little fantasy. Surely I can afford to be more generous than this. Still, as the plane moves on, it almost feels as if a small piece of me tears itself away and remains behind, suspended in the air above the clouds, unwilling to leave.

An hour later, we land at Tan Son Nhut airfield. Once one of the busiest airports in the world, it is now only a shadow of its former self. Dozens of old concrete revetments stand empty, and tall grass grows up through the cracks at the edge of the tarmac. In one corner of the field is an aircraft graveyard filled with the rusting stripped-down hulks of American military aircraft. Intense heat slaps me in the face the moment I step from the plane. In Hanoi, the weather has been cool and overcast; here in the south, it is the peak of the dry season.

We are met at the terminal by Le Kieu, director of the war crimes exhibit in Ho Chi Minh City, a Miss Phuong, who is Mr. Kieu's assistant, Xuan Giai, General Chi's "advance man" who came down a few days earlier to arrange our southern itinerary, and Doan Duc Luu, our new interpreter. After the introductions are made, Mr. Luu tells us that we must check in at our hotel, then we will meet again in the afternoon. He escorts us to a large black late-1960s Chevrolet sedan, and we are off.

Along the road into the city, we pass the old headquarters of Military Assistance Command Vietnam, once the nerve center for all American forces in Vietnam. A nearby roadsign pointing the way to "MACV HQ" is still clearly visible, if old and faded. Mr. Luu tells us that

the bridge we are crossing is the place where Nguyen Van Troi was captured by Saigon police while trying to blow up Secretary of Defense
Robert McNamara with a bomb in 1964. Troi, a 19-year-old student, was
executed by a firing squad a few months later. "Down with the
Americans!" were his last words, "Long live Ho Chi Minh!"

We pass the old American embassy, then the old Presidential
Palace, once the home of Ngo Dinh Diem, Nguyen Cao Ky and Nguyen
Van Thieu, and finally the "Pink Cathedral," its name derived from its
distinctive bricks. John and Bruce both spent time in Saigon during the
war, and they eagerly share their recollections, recognizing this building
and that intersection. In spite of my best efforts, I find myself depressed
and resentful that they are seeing at least a part of their past while I will
not see so much as a brick or a blade of grass to help me close the circle
of my memories. I am ashamed of my pettiness, but I cannot make the
disappointment go away.

After our cramped rides around Hanoi in the little green Toyota, the
sprawling room in the big old Chevy is a real treat. But I recall McAuliff
warning that we would have to pay for ground transportation in Vietnam. "I think we're paying for this car," I point out. John and Bruce say
no, we didn't pay for our car in Hanoi. "But that was the general's personal car," I remind them. Relax, they tell me, we would have been told
about it if they expected us to pay.

As we ride through the streets, physical differences between north
and south are immediately apparent. Much of the older French architecture has been supplanted by newer American-style buildings. In Hanoi,
things have been deteriorating for forty years. Here, it has only been ten
years. And though one could hardly say that motor vehicles are
numerous, compared to Hanoi, Ho Chi Minh City is a madhouse of
buses, three-wheeled Lambrettas, motorbikes and motorscooters—all
whizzing along amid the more familiar crush of bicycles and pedestrians.
Pollution-control devices are unheard of, and the air reeks with the acid
sting of burnt fumes. Compared to the sedate calm of Hanoi, Ho Chi
Minh City is a boisterous, jarring cacophony.

Our hotel is the Cuu Long—Nine Dragons—once the Frenchified
and aristocratic Majestic. It faces the Saigon River at the foot of a street
called Dong Koi, or Uprising. In the time of the Americans, the street
was called Tu Do, or Freedom. "The Saigonese have a joke about this
street," Mr. Luu tells us as we pull to a stop in front of the hotel, "They
say that after the uprising, there is no freedom." He laughs, then perhaps
realizing that he doesn't know yet whether or not we can be trusted, he

quickly adds, "Please don't quote me." He tells us to meet him here again at 1 p.m.

Once again, as in Hanoi, John and Bruce will share one room while I will have a room to myself. Despite feeling like the odd man out, I try to remind myself that it is the most sensible arrangement because Bruce has the least money and John's hotel bill will be covered by his university. To my dismay, however, I discover that our hosts have reserved for us business-class suites, each suite with a two-bed bedroom, a furnished sittingroom, and a full bathroom. Can't the three of us share one suite, I ask the hotel clerk. No, I am told. Can we get smaller rooms, I ask. No, I am told, it is the Christmas season and the hotel is completely full. Only then do I notice the decorated Christmas tree in the lobby. I had almost forgotten that tomorrow is Christmas Day.

Eighteen years ago, when I was 19, I had spent a Christmas in Vietnam. We had just come down to Quang Tri after 33 mud-soaked days at Con Thien, and I had spent that Christmas Eve sitting on top of a lonely hill, dreaming of home and watching red and green flares exploding all along the DMZ in a riotously forlorn celebration of the birth of Christ. I had wanted so much not to be where I was. Did I want it as badly as I wanted it now? Time plays funny tricks with memory, and immediate pain is always so much more vivid and real.

At least the air conditioning works, I discover later as I unpack in my enormous, empty, three-room suite, and I won't have to trot down the hall every time I need to urinate in the middle of the night. Even the hotel elevators work. I wonder how much these luxuries are costing me, and if I can afford them. And that goddamned big car. What will I do if I actually run out of money?

The room has a telephone. So did my room at the Thong Nhat, but it didn't work. I pick this one up and try it, reaching the clerk at the front desk. Can I call the United States from here, I ask. Yes, I am told — much to my surprise — what number would I like? Excitedly, I give her my home phone number in Philadelphia. In a few minutes, I am actually speaking with Anne! It is nearly midnight back home, almost Christmas Day. Anne is fine, she tells me; in the morning, she will go up to my parents' home in Perkasie for the day. I tell her that I am fine, that I won't be able to go to central Vietnam, but that otherwise the trip is going well. I tell her I miss her. I don't tell her how disappointed I am that I can't go anywhere I had wanted to, that I am worrying about all the things that could happen before I can get home again. I tell her I love her, and I hang up.

I am sitting on the bed trying to keep from crying when the telephone rings. It is the hotel clerk. "Four and a half minutes," she says, "$47.40." Payable in U.S. dollars, of course. So much for calling Anne again.

John and Bruce come by the room and we walk around the corner to a little restaurant to eat lunch. As we order, the man next to us asks in English where we are from. When we tell him the United States, he tells us that he studied English at the university in Saigon in 1973 and 1974. Now he is a translator of Russian documents. We ask him what he thinks of the new regime. He laughs softly — a sort of short, choked sigh. "I don't get involved in politics," he replies. When we get up to leave, the man leans over to us again. "They will know I've been talking to you," he says. "When I get back to work, they will question me. I'll tell them I was helping you with the menu." He laughs again and shrugs his shoulders. "You say you are writers," he adds; "you will understand what I say, and what I don't say."

Luu and the big black Chevy are waiting back at the hotel, and we drive to the war crimes exhibit where the others are waiting. Faced with the strain of having to get to know a whole new entourage, I find myself missing Mrs. Troan, Mr. Hoang and Loan. As we drink iced coffee and eat breadfruit, we try to get to know these people. Miss Phuong is in her late 20s or early 30s and is married, though I notice that even her colleagues address her as "Miss," perhaps because of her young age. She is unusual in that she is slightly plump. I have not seen too many overweight people in Vietnam. Mr. Giai, a former soldier, is missing his left thumb; he is thin and frail, perhaps in his 70s, barely five feet tall, but his eyes shine with vitality. Mr. Luu is 29 and learned English while studying in Hungary for four years; he works for the Foreign Ministry, but has been "borrowed" for the week by the commission. Mr. Kieu is about General Chi's age and is also a veteran. Thirty years ago, he and the general served together. "Because the earth is round, we meet again," he says, patting the general on the knee.

Mr. Giai asks for our passports and visas. Again, I am reluctant to part with mine, but there is nothing to be done except to turn them over and hope I will see them again. General Chi outlines our agenda for the coming week. Then he tells us we are free for the rest of the day. He suggests that we might want to go to Christmas Mass at the Pink Cathedral that evening, telling us that religion is still permitted under the new regime. "Communism can coexist with religion," he says. "The streets will be crowded tonight; be careful of your wallets," he warns us.

"Pickpockets." He gestures apologetically. "Twenty years of American influence," he adds, though we had gotten a similar warning from Loan in the marketplace in Old Hanoi.

We climb back into the car and Luu asks us if there is anywhere special we want to go. Bruce asks if we can go to the Cholon Market. On the way there, we pass another cathedral where Diem and his brother Ngo Dinh Nhu tried to hide the night they were overthrown in November 1963 by a U.S.-sanctioned military coup. They were caught and shot by people who turned out to be no better than they were, and they were nothing to brag about.

Luu asks us about our previous time in Vietnam, and he learns that all three of us had been wounded. He asks about our wounds. When we tell him we were all wounded by shrapnel, searching hard to find and show him our small, faded scars, he turns away abruptly, as if to say: I thought you meant you were *wounded*. At first, I am angry and amazed at his insensitivity, but as we ride on I think of Nguyen Van Hung, the one-armed veteran in Hanoi, and it dawns on me that no one in a country like Vietnam can be expected to take our red badges of courage very seriously.

On a street corner in front of the market, I see my first Amerasian child, a boy of 13 or 14 with reddish-brown hair. He makes no attempt to communicate with me, but follows me steadily with his eyes, almost as if he is trying to see himself in me. I smile, but he doesn't smile back.

On the way back to the hotel, I cannot restrain myself any longer. "Are we paying for this car?" I ask Luu. He looks at me, mildly dumbfounded.

"Of course," he says. I look at Bruce and John, and they stare back. We try to explain that it must seem odd for Americans to be pleading poverty, but that it cost a lot of money to get here at all and we really don't have a lot of spare change. Might it be possible, we ask, to get a smaller, less expensive car? He's not sure, he replies; he'll have to discuss it with the general. He drops us at the hotel, telling us to be ready to go at eight o'clock the next morning.

It is still early, not yet suppertime, and we decide to go for a walk. Like Hanoi, Ho Chi Minh City seems blanketed in a perpetual sheen of dust, but the bright sun—even in late afternoon—makes everything seem lighter and newer than it is. On the balconies and terraces of nearly every building, flowering plants splash bright bursts of color everywhere: yellows, reds, purples and pinks. On Nguyen Hue Boulevard, we are greeted by the remarkable spectacle of two long rows of American cars parked along either curb. All date from the late 1950s and early 1960s: Plymouths, Dodges, Chryslers, Fords, Chevvies, even an Edsel and a Packard and a couple of Studebakers. They have big fins and Flash Gordon grills, and they are all painted two-tone red and white. Though they will be there every day in the coming week, we never see anyone driving them, and we never do learn why they are there or what they are used for.

As we walk, we are followed by half a dozen cyclo-drivers, all calling brashly in English for our business. It does no good to tell them we want to walk; they follow after us anyway, block after block, calling, "Maybe tomorrow, maybe tonight, you ride with me." A handful of children follow after us, too, asking for money and cigarettes. John and Bruce assure me that this is nothing like Saigon in the old days—when Tu Do Street was lined with bars and prostitutes, and drugs were sold openly in the streets, and the beggars and cripples and "Saigon Cowboys" (ARVN deserters and street punks) were as thick as molasses—but after the quiet dignity of Hanoi, the brassy attention we are receiving makes me very uncomfortable. It was fun to walk in Hanoi; it isn't fun here.

On the sidewalk in front of one shop, imbedded in a tile mosaic, I notice the words "Rue Catinat." I remember the street from Graham Greene's novel, *The Quiet American*, but I had not realized that it was the same street later renamed Tu Do and finally Dong Koi. "That's where Graham Greene used to live," says John, pointing down a side street. We turn and walk until we are standing in front of a three-story, dirty, cream-colored structure wedged in between the buildings on either side of it. The building is nondescript, and there is nothing to indicate that the famous British novelist had ever lived here.

The Quiet American is one of my all-time favorite books, a remarkable and sad little novel published in 1955 but written a year or two earlier, around the time—or perhaps even before—the French finally gave up and quit Vietnam. Fully a decade before the vast American build-up, as the French floundered in the mire of their Indochinese colonies, Greene had strolled the Rue Catinat and sipped crème de cassis at the streetside bar of the Hotel Majestic, and like a weary prophet, he had seen the whole American disaster approaching.

"Why don't you go away, Pyle, without causing trouble?" Greene's alter-ego, a British journalist named Fowler, says to the newly arrived eager, young American CIA operative, "You and your kind are trying to make a war with the help of people who just aren't interested."

"They don't want communism," Pyle replies.

"They want enough rice," says Fowler. "They don't want to be shot at. They want one day to be much the same as another. They don't want our white skins around telling them what they want."

But it was just a novel, and it was 1953, and Pyle and his kind knew better. And now, more than thirty years later, Pyle and his kind can be found in places like Nicaragua and El Salvador and Honduras.

Not far from Greene's old apartment is a small plaza. I recognize it immediately as the setting for Horace Coleman's poem, "A Black Soldier Remembers":

My Saigon daughter I saw only once
standing in the dusty square
across from the Brinks BOQ/PX
in back of the National Assembly
next to the ugly statue of
the crouching marines facing
the fish pond the VC blew up
during Tet.

The amputee beggars watch us.
The same color and the same eyes.
She does not offer me one of the
silly hats she sells Americans and
I have nothing she needs but
the sad smile she already has.

There is the old Brinks BOQ/PX. There is the old National Assembly, now a public theater. The ugly statue is gone, torn down in a fit of rage and joy in the first hours after the liberation — or the fall of Saigon, depending on one's point of view — but the concrete pedestal remains. In place of Coleman's Saigon daughter is a small boy, full-blooded Vietnamese, selling chunks of raw sugarcane from a flat reed basket. Born after the Americans finally left, he finds us a curious and fascinating novelty. Further on, a shopkeeper motions us into his store. He asks if we want to change money: 110 dong to the dollar.

Like the menu at the Thong Nhat Hotel restaurant, the menu at the Cuu Long is limited and unchanging from day to day. But the Cuu Long restaurant is located on the top floor of the hotel, and its large picture windows afford a magnificent view of the great ox-bow that gives Saigon its name: Bend in the River. In the late afternoon, small ferries scurry back and forth from one riverbank to the other, carrying people home from work. Several large deepwater ships are tied up just down the river from the hotel, and upriver I can see the booms and derricks of the American-built shipyard at New Port. Below us, a block away, children splash in the fountain pool beneath a huge statue of the ancient Vietnamese general, Tran Hung Dao. Five floors down, the streets are already beginning to fill with people.

Christmas Eve is a kind of Mardi Gras time in Ho Chi Minh City. As evening comes on, the streets become jam-packed with noisy throngs hurling confetti and milling about aimlessly. We try to walk to the Pink Cathedral, but it is impossible even to get close to the church. I've never liked crowds anyway, and I'm not exactly in a holiday spirit, so I leave John and Bruce to fend for themselves and go back to the hotel.

But there is nothing to do at the hotel. This would have been Anne's and my first Christmas together in our first real home after a succession of cramped apartments. So there she is, alone in an empty house. And here I am, alone in an empty hotel room half a world away.

Christmas Day

Luu and the general are waiting for us in the hotel lobby, but the big black Chevy is nowhere to be seen. Instead, General Chi apologizes profusely for the arrangements his staff has made without consulting us. Again, we explain how awkward it is for us to suggest that we are poor when we can see all around us what it means to be truly poor. But he dismisses our explanation with a wave of the hand. "I did not understand how much you have sacrificed in order to visit us," he says via Luu, "We have some strange notions about Americans. We have much to learn. This is a lesson for me. I thank you for your willingness to speak honestly."

Luu explains that the general has arranged to borrow a car from the city government for the day. Soon it arrives — a small, white Toyota — and all five of us pile in with the driver. Mr. Kieu, Mr. Giai and Miss Phuong are waiting for us at the war crimes exhibit. Over tea and fruit, Mr. Giai returns our passports and visas — much to my relief. He does not explain where they have been, but I assume that we've been registered with the local police. At least we didn't have to show up in person this time.

Two young women in *ao dais* walk into the reception room and greet us. They are sisters, we are told: Thieu Thi Tao and Thieu Thi Tan. Both were arrested by the Thieu regime in 1968 — Miss Tao at age 18, Miss Tan at age 15 — and held for six years. Miss Tao walks with a barely noticeable limp, but is full-fleshed, cheerful and quietly charming. Her sister, however, is thin and sallow; she walks with a heavy limp and seems to have trouble concentrating on our conversation. For the most part, she does not participate in it.

The exhibit itself turns out to be rather different from what I had expected. The war with the United States is the subject of several rooms, but there are also rooms dealing with the old regime, Pol Pot, the Chinese invasion of 1979, several post-1975 internal "reactionary" plots, and post-1975 spying and infiltration operations sponsored by the Chinese and the Thais. "It is important to educate younger generations," says General Chi, explaining that they hope to add exhibits dealing with colonial France, fascist Japan and Chiang Kai Chek's Taiwan. "Our purpose is not to foster hatred of past enemies, but to teach the consequences of war in order to prevent such things from happening in the future."

Part of the United States exhibit is a wall-mounted glass display case containing various kinds of rock-and-roll paraphernalia: Black Sabbath T-shirts, Iron Maiden posters, album jackets from heavy metal, acid-rock and punk-rock bands — the sorts of things one might find in any American department store. The captions are all in Vietnamese.

"What's this stuff here for?" I ask Luu.

"That's supposed to be examples of the decadent influence of Western culture," he replies, shrugging his shoulders sheepishly.

"I know a lot of parents of American teenagers who would agree," I respond, laughing.

"They used to have copies of *Playboy* magazines here, too," Luu says, "but the exhibit was too popular, so they took them out."

The next exhibit is more sobering, however: a display of maps, and photographs depicting chemical defoliation and its impact on the environment. Some of the photos are of badly deformed children, and there are even some horribly deformed fetuses in bottles. The Vietnamese claim — not without reason — that Agent Orange and other dioxins used in defoliation have led to a high incidence of birth defects and diseases. It is a claim made also by many former American soldiers and their families. American chemical companies have consistently denied any correlation, and the American government has offered only token assistance to its former soldiers. Meanwhile, large areas of Vietnam were blanketed with chemical defoliants during the war. And the bottled fetuses here are the lucky ones: they were born dead or never brought to term. The unlucky ones live in a special hospital we are scheduled to visit this afternoon.

Outside, in the courtyard, are various pieces of hardware: a French guillotine still used by Diem as late as 1961, an American tank, a 175-millimeter "Long Tom" cannon, a "Daisy Cutter" bomb casing. There is also a full scale replica of a "tiger cage," a particularly inhuman type of prison cell used by the Saigon regime at Con Son Prison Island. Con Son made the headlines in the early 1970s when a man named Don Luce revealed the existence of the tiger cages to the United States Congress and the media.

Luce is an interesting man. A solid middleclass farmer from upstate New York, he went to Vietnam in 1958 as a civilian agricultural advisor. He ended up staying for over a dozen years, learning as much about Vietnam and the Vietnamese as any Westerner alive, and along the way turning against the U.S. war and committing his life — literally — to putting a stop to it.

"You know Don?" Miss Tao asks in English as we stand looking at the tiger cage.

"Yes," I reply, "I just saw him last August, in fact."

"Please tell him I'm doing well," she says. "He helped my family many times."

"Were you a Viet Cong?" I ask.

"Oh, yes," she replies, "I began working here in Saigon for the revolution when I was very young, and I was a party member." She explains that she had been a student at the well-to-do Madame Curie High School, and that she had been betrayed by another student. At one time or another, her entire family had been imprisoned by the old regime, but none of them had ever admitted their party ties.

She points to the tiger cage, a 4 × 8 foot cell with concrete walls and bars only in the ceiling. "I was kept in one of these for three years," she says. "Often, there were five or six of us to each cell. We were seldom allowed any clothing, and guards would come at all hours of the day or night and throw cold water or excrement on us. Sometimes, a kind jailer would give us a bit of meat or fish. Once, a guard gave me a small hot pepper — I remember it so well — it tasted sweet, like candy. But that didn't happy very often. Even the sympathetic guards were afraid to be kind; if they got caught, they would end up as prisoners, too. Most of the guards were very cruel. One time, they threw a phosphorous grenade into our cell, setting us on fire. Water wouldn't stop the burning, but I poured urine on myself and the acid in the urine put the fire out." She speaks in an even, gentle voice. If there is bitterness or anger inside, the voice does not reveal it.

"How did you keep from going mad?" I ask.

"I pretended to be far away," she replies, smiling. "They couldn't lock up my imagination. I knew we would win." She explains that she and her sister were finally released in 1974. "For my sister, maybe it was too late." I glance around and spot Miss Tan standing alone by the door to the reception room. She has not accompanied us on our tour of the exhibit. "She tires easily now," says Miss Tao. "Her health is not good. She cannot work at all."

"Doesn't it make you angry sometimes?" I ask.

"We did what we had to," she replies. "Many people sacrificed. Many people. But that was the past. You know, only a few months ago, I met one of my former guards here in Saigon"—she says Saigon, not Ho Chi Minh City. "He was walking down the street and he passed right by me, but he didn't recognize me. I almost spoke to him, but I didn't want him to be frightened."

"He's free?" I ask, incredulous.

Oh, yes, she explains, many of her former tormenters have been re-educated and are now free.

"And it doesn't bother you?" I ask.

"That's not important anymore," she replies firmly. "We can't afford to be vindictive. If we do not have successful national reconciliation, history has taught us that we will end up as a province of China."

General Chi approaches and puts his arm around Miss Tao, giving her a fatherly hug. "Miss Tao is a symbol of the new Vietnam," he says, "She still shows the effects of her hardship, but she is succeeding by hard work. Did she tell you she graduated from the university in biology?"

Back in the reception room, I notice that Miss Tan is gone. Mr. Kieu asks us if we have any questions. I ask about the Cao Dai, a religious sect centered in Tay Ninh Province. My understanding is that the Cao Dai were anti–American, but the exhibit suggests otherwise. Mr. Kieu says that Cao Dai opposition to the United States was "only a ruse," that in fact they were supported by the CIA. After the liberation, he says, the Cao Dai revealed themselves as antirevolutionaries.

How do they explain the so-called "boat people," we ask.

There are five types of boat people, we are told: former members of the old regime, the bourgeousie who profitted off the United States presence, people who made their living off wartime services, ethnic Chinese, and a much smaller group of artists and other civilians. Many of these people could not integrate into the new society. Some, accustomed to power and privilege, resented having to work for a living. Some committed crimes in former times and were afraid of the consequences. Many were affected by the sudden drop in their standard of living when the false economy created by American aid and the American presence dried up. Others who left went to join relatives already living abroad. And still others were influenced by the Voice of America and other American and Chinese propaganda.

"Talk to the boat people in the United States about why they left," says General Chi. "They understand why they left better than we do."

"We feel very sorry for the suffering of the boat people," says Mr. Kieu. Western propaganda led many to believe that they would be rescued by American ships as soon as they reached international waters, he says, but instead they had to face long voyages in unseaworthy boats, piracy, storms and thirst. Many received letters and goods from the West designed to make them think that life would be easy, but now they cannot even get out of the squalid refugee camps where they are kept as virtual prisoners. Furthermore, he adds, Western aid sent by well-meaning people ends up in the wrong hands. In Thailand, refugee aid is supervised by the Thai military, and actually ends up in the hands of the Thai military and the forces of Pol Pot.

In any case, says Mr. Kieu, the number of boat people has declined markedly in recent years. Except for criminals, people who wish to leave may do so under the Orderly Departure Program. Vietnam has given a list of 40,000 approved emigrants to the United Nations High Commission on Refugees, he says, though only 10,000 have left so far because of conditions imposed by the United States.

Next we ask about Truong Nhu Tang, a founder of the southern National Liberation Front — the political arm of the VC — and the former Minister of Justice in the Provisional Revolutionary Government, who defected to the West in 1978. His book, *A Viet Cong Memoir*, is a scathing criticism of the new regime, charging that the northern leadership used the southern revolutionaries to seize power, then took control of the south, pushing aside the old NLF/PRG leadership and running the south like an occupied state.

To begin with, the general responds, the distinction between north and south has never been more than a fantasy imposed upon the Vietnamese by outsiders; there is and always has been only one Vietnam. He points out that many of the most powerful leaders of the old regime — Diem, Ky and Thieu, among others — were actually born in the north; Diem was born in the same province as Ho Chi Minh. "My own wife is a southerner," he reminds us; "what does it matter?"

But during the war, hadn't the DRV (North Vietnam) repeatedly insisted that reunification with the south would be done only gradually over a period of years? Yet a unified Vietnam had been declared only a little over a year after the war ended. How is this explained, we ask. Because the people wanted rapid reunification, we are told.

What about the charges in Tang's book, we ask.

"The book is just his way of making a living," the general responds. "He has to earn a living somehow."

But why did he leave, we ask.

He wanted more power than he had, we are told; he wanted to be more important than he was. "Things are not perfect, it's true," says Mr. Kieu, "but things can never be perfect." Both Chi and Kieu suggest that Tang was "a bad apple in the barrel." After his defection, they say, Tang went to China to help the Chinese plan their 1979 invasion of Vietnam.

John asks about Ong Dao Dua, the man known as "the Coconut Monk." Dua is, or was, the leader of a small religious sect located on Phoenix Island in the Mekong Delta, the place where John collected many of his *ca dao*, and John had known him during the war. He has heard that Dua was arrested after the war and is still being held. Yes, he is under arrest, we are told. But Dua ran for president in 1971 against Thieu, John argues; he was vocally opposed to the United States and the Saigon regime, and constantly in trouble for it. That was all a subterfuge, we are told; he was a traitor and a CIA agent.

What about the re-education camps, we ask. Of course, they have had to re-educate many people after so many years of French and American rule, General Chi says, but the new regime has treated these people far better than most countries in similar circumstances. He cites the fact that the French executed many collaborators after World War Two. Mr. Kieu adds that five of his cousins had worked for the old regime and were sent to re-education camps. They told him that the food was bad, he says, but that they were not tortured, and all were eventually released. "My cousins are not committed to the revolution," he says, "but they recognize the same fatherland as I do."

Riding back to the hotel, John says there is no way on earth that the Coconut Monk could have been a CIA agent. Though their explanation for the boat people was very detailed and fairly convincing, their offhanded dismissal of the Cao Dai, Truong Nhu Tang and Ong Dao Dua leaves much to be desired. It is as if they cannot understand dissent except in terms of "reactionaries, traitors and outside influences." Am I really surprised by that, I wonder. No, I suppose not.

I am not going to the hospital for Agent Orange victims, I tell Bruce and John over lunch. I have read much of the literature on Agent Orange. I understand its consequences. But this morning's exhibit is all I can bear to see in terms of tangible evidence. I do not have the stomach to spend an afternoon with horribly deformed children. Call it cowardice, or guilt, or whatever one will—I know my limit, and that exceeds it. When Luu comes to pick us up, I tell him I am not feeling well, and John and Bruce graciously support my lie.

Instead, I decide to go for a walk. But the moment I step out of the hotel, the cyclo drivers are on me, following me down the street, calling after me. A red-haired Amerasian cyclo driver tells me his name is Jimmy. He claims to know who his father is and wants me to deliver a letter to him. Where does his father live, I ask. "Texas," he says. Where in Texas, I ask. "Texas," he says again. Another cyclo driver, a full-blooded Vietnamese, says his father is living in the United States. He wants to join him there. Will I help him?

There are always winners and losers, I tell myself, and these are some of the losers. I knew they would be here, but it is hard to deal with them in the flesh. I walk back to the hotel and take a nap. When John and Bruce return, I ask them how it was.

"You made the right decision," says Bruce.

"Pretty grim, huh?" I say.

"Pretty grim," says John.

In the evening, we go with Luu and Miss Phuong to the old National Assembly to hear a concert. We are still hoping to hear some traditional Vietnamese music, and Luu has told us that's what this will be, but once again it turns out to be Socialist Realism Rock, and I am now convinced that no one in Vietnam understands the meaning of the English word "traditional." Among the songs performed are "Marching to Saigon" and "Springtime on the Oil Rig." Is it my imagination, or is Luu having trouble keeping a straight face as he translates the titles for me?

Thursday, December 26

General Tran Thien Khiem had been a powerbroker in the old Saigon regime. He had once saved Ngo Dinh Diem from an attempted coup, had later participated in the coup that ousted Diem, and had played various roles in the multiple short-lived governments that followed until Nguyen Cao Ky finally consolidated power in 1965. He had subsequently served as Vietnam's ambassador to the United States. According to various American and Vietnamese sources, he was also one of the top ringleaders of the illegal Saigon heroin trade — a network that involved, says historian Stanley Karnow, "nearly every prominent member of the Saigon regime," reaping millions of dollars in profit from the misery and addiction of his own people and American GIs alike.

As we pull into the courtyard of the building that houses Ho Chi Minh City's Culture and Information Service — this time riding in a green car borrowed from who knows where — John tells Bruce and me that this is the same building where he had once met General Khiem in the late 1960s. As John tells it, Khiem was then Minister of the Interior and John was field representative for the Committee of Responsibility to Save War-Injured Children. John was having difficulty obtaining exit visas for a number of children badly in need of medical care in the United States, and some of the children were on the verge of death. The Saigon regime didn't like to release these children because it was tantamount to admitting that they couldn't take care of their own.

"How will I look if I release these children to an antiwar group?" Khiem had responded to John's request.

"How will you look if these children die?" John had replied. Khiem had granted the exit visas.

We are met inside by a Mr. Truc and a Mr. Thu. As we are served tea, breadfruit and tangerines, the two men present us with 1986 calendars. Above each month is a studio portrait of a different Vietnamese woman—all of them young and very beautiful. "We are communists," says General Chi, "but we also like to be happy; beauty is welcomed everywhere."

Mr. Thu tells us that the population of Ho Chi Minh City is 3.5 million. A million and a half in 1954, it had swollen by the end of the war to over four million. "Many people were forced into the cities from the countryside by the old regime," he says. I know this to be true. On the theory that the guerrillas were "the fish" and the civilian population was "the sea," the idea was to dry up the sea in order to suffocate the fish. Carrying the benign name of "Forced Draft Urbanization," the program translated in reality into a systematic effort to make life in the countryside so intolerable through the use of bombing and other military operations that people would be forced to move to the cities.

After the war, he tells us, the problem became how to move as many people as possible back to the countryside and how to find jobs for those who remained. Many people were "encouraged" to go to so-called New Economic Zones—critics charge that these people were forced to go, but I have no way of evaluating that accusation—where state farms were carved out of land left fallow by the war. In Ho Chi Minh City itself, each district and ward has a handicraft center where people produce light goods like reed chairs and soccer balls, but unemployment and under-employment, Mr. Thu tells us, is still a major problem. Many of the unemployed, he says, are among the half-million former "puppet" soldiers who took off their uniforms and melted into the city on Libera-tion Day.

That was a great day, says Mr. Truc, who explains that he and Mr. Thu had both spent years in the VC underground in Saigon during the war. He doesn't call it "the war," but rather "the struggle for national sal-vation." When the "Liberation Army" approached Saigon, he says, the people welcomed them. Their refusal to fight against the liberation army was, in effect, a "popular uprising," a mass revolt against the old regime. "It is a pity that you were not here to see it with your own eyes," he says.

Here, too, we ask about the re-education camps. Very few enlisted men were required to go to the camps, we are told. Most were asked merely to identify themselves, after which they could go home. Only high ranking officers were sent to the camps, most for periods of one to three years. And there were no executions; Chi, Truc and Thu are all very emphatic about that. Only a very limited number of people remain in the camps now, we are told, about 7,000. "We do not care what people were," says Mr. Thu. "The important thing is how they behave now."

"Ho Chi Minh said that if you want to build a socialist society," says Mr. Truc, "you must build a socialist man." He says that the new regime has spent much time and energy trying to instill discipline, self-sacrifice, responsibility and love for others. "We have still far to go," he says, "but ten years is a short time, and we are making progress."

"Rebuilding our culture after the war has been a very heavy burden," says Mr. Thu. Thousands of drug addicts have had to be rehabilitated. Former prostitutes have had to be provided with medical treatment and vocational training in such skills as weaving and sewing. The sudden end to 30 years of a false war economy bolstered by American aid and imported material goods has caused a significant drop in the standard of living. The major problem, he says, is how to convert Ho Chi Minh City from a consumer city to a producer city. Because much of the city and the surrounding countryside was destroyed during the war, there are also problems with rebuilding, as well as difficulties with old bomb craters and unexploded mines.

Is it true, we ask, that former ARVN soldiers have been forced to look for and dig up old mines? All three men deny this vigorously. It is done by experts from the liberation army, they insist; reports to the contrary are absolutely untrue. It is also untrue, Mr. Thu adds, that former prostitutes have been forced to marry disabled veterans; this, too, he says, is Western propaganda.

What does the Culture and Information Service actually do, we ask. We are told that it is responsible for the arts, recreation, literature, libraries and newspapers within a 50-kilometer radius of the city. There are 60 theaters in Ho Chi Minh City, but there are still not enough in more rural areas. They are trying to establish a "balance of access" for city and rural people, Mr. Truc says, including the development of traveling performance groups and mobile libraries to reach out into the countryside.

It is also the responsibility of the Service to "oppose the invasion of Western culture," he says—not just from the United States, but from England, France, Japan and other countries as well. He specifically mentions rock-and-roll and its "bad influence on youth." Moreover, he says, the Service must work to counter the "insidious influence" of Vietnamese refugee publications coming from the West.

Not all elements of Western culture are rejected, General Chi reminds us. "Progressive influences" are welcomed—he cites my anthology *Carrying the Darkness* as an example of a progressive influence—it is only the "reactionary influences" that are being rejected.

"Of course," says Mr. Thu, "we have not shut the door." The desired goal is to combine a socialist culture with a nationalist culture. He mentions that the Vietnamese are actively seeking international cultural exchange, and expresses the desire to send Vietnamese performers to the U.S. "We want the world to understand Vietnamese culture," he says.

As we are leaving, Mr. Truc asks us what we think of Ronald Reagan's massive military build-up, mentioning in particular the American nuclear arsenal. He makes no mention of Soviet nuclear capability, but he sends us off with the admonition that "if there is nuclear war, there will be no winners."

At lunchtime, John takes Bruce and me to a restaurant he used to frequent when he lived in Saigon. The proprietor is a middle-aged woman who doesn't recognize John immediately. A grown daughter is with her, and John points to the daughter's leg. "You have a scar there, don't you?" he asks, "You were burned by a hot motorcycle muffler pipe when you were fourteen, weren't you?" Mother and daughter suddenly remember: John had been in the restaurant when the incident had happened.

Their joy at seeing an old friend is tempered by fear, however. The mother shows us to a table, then sits down at the table next to us. The shop is nearly deserted. She looks around furtively as she talks, stopping frequently. John explains that she used to work at the United States embassy. "Look out for the cyclo drivers," she warns us, "They're all secret police. The police are everywhere. They will check your hotel room. They know everything."

"How are you getting along?" John asks.

"Very bad," she says, shrugging and frowning. "They took away my food license. Now I can only sell soda, coffee and tea." She explains that she and her family of five have been trying to leave for six years. "Can you help us?" she asks. She gets up, goes behind the counter, and returns with a piece of paper. It is a letter from the United States Immigration Service apparently approving them for the Orderly Departure Program. It is three years old. "We can't get exit visas," she says.

John writes down the ODP number, though all three of us know there is little or nothing we can do. "You should go now," she says. She draws a single finger horizontally across her throat. "Watch out for the cyclo drivers."

Nguyen Van Thieu lives in quiet seclusion in London. Nguyen Ngoc Loan, the infamous former police chief of Saigon, runs a restaurant in

suburban Washington, D.C. Nguyen Cao Ky owns a liquor store in
southern California — and according to some allegations, heads a sha-
dowy ring of refugee extortionists and criminals known as the Vietnamese Mafia. The rich and the powerful got out. The junior lieutenants
and faithful servants got left behind.

Our first stop of the afternoon is the Rehabilitation Center for
Malnourished Orphans. The director is Nguyen Thi Mai, a middle-aged
woman with a firm handshake and a steady gaze. Over coffee, water-
melon and freshly cooked spring rolls, she tells us that during the war she
was a VC political cadre organizing peace demonstrations in "the enemy
zone" — territory controlled by the old regime.

Then she explains that before liberation, the rehabilitation center
used to be run by Catholic nuns, and many of the nuns are still on the
staff. The center accepts newborn babies up to the age of three, providing
24-hour care for 150-200 infants at a time with a staff of 60. The center
also provides an out-patient clinic for poor families, professional training
for other medical personnel, and medical assistance to New Economic
Zones in the surrounding countryside.

Inside the main hospital building, a group of three-year-olds is having lunch. Most of them are clearly frightened of us, but one little fellow
in a blue shirt and incongruous conical clown's hat quietly walks over to
me, takes my hand, and proceeds to join our tour. In other rooms are
dozens of cribs, each containing an infant. Many of them are crying or
rocking rhythmically as white-uniformed nurses move among them.
Mrs. Mai picks up one infant, gently rubbing its back and kissing it.

"They don't get held enough," she sighs, putting the infant back
in its crib, bending over and kissing it one more time. "We do the best
we can, but there are not enough of us to go around. Money is a constant
problem."

What happens to these children, we ask. Most of them are eventually adopted, she says. Since the end of the war, over a thousand of
them have been placed with families. It is the best news I have heard all
day.

At the People's Committee for District 10, we are met by committee Vice President Truong Tan Bien. He greets us expansively, once again
explicitly making the distinction between the "American warmongers"
and the "progressive American people." He explains that there are 18
districts in and around Ho Chi Minh City, with 18 wards to each district.
The People's Committee is, apparently, simply the government; there
are people's committees at the ward, district and province levels.

District 10, he says, is 5.6 square kilometers and has a population of 200,000. During "the American war of aggression," the district was half slums and half ARVN and American military bases; there were no recreation, education, medical or production facilities. Though they still have "many difficulties" — a phrase I am growing weary of hearing, though undoubtedly it is true — he says the district is making great progress in refurbishing old buildings and constructing new ones, developing schools and handicraft industries. All construction is done locally by local labor, and rent is subsidized.

Then he takes us on a tour of several new residential construction sites. One consists of several rows of two-story, townhouse-type apartments, the other is a complex of several multistory apartment buildings. Some of the buildings are occupied, others are still under construction. There is a medical symbol hanging from one of the apartment buildings, and Mr. Bien explains that each building has a small clinic.

All of these buildings are much more attractive than the concrete slab–style apartments we saw under construction in Hanoi. "They know how to build buildings down here," General Chi says to me, taking me by the arm and pointing at one of the finished apartment buildings. "You Americans taught them how to build. Up north . . ." He completes his sentence with a shrug and an almost quizzical little smile. How is it, I wonder, that in ten years' time southern technological skills have not managed to find their way north?

But just as I am about to ask, we are bundled back into the cars and taken to Ky Hoa Lake Park. Mr. Bien explains that the park has been built since the end of the war on land that used to be marshes and swamps. The park is full of people, young and old. The lake itself is occupied by an armada of rowboats and paddleboats. There are also small amusement rides for children — one consists of tanks and airplanes that go round and round — monkeys and cats in cages, kiosks selling toys and snacks, and tables in green glades for picnics. The park is colorful and bright, and children race by us laughing and shouting.

On the way back to the hotel, we pass a bus with large lettering on the side that reads: Saigon Tourism. The ashtrays at the hotel say the same thing. I have also noticed that almost everyone, even the "Party types," seems to use "Saigon" and "Ho Chi Minh City" interchangeably. I ask Luu about this. "Ho Chi Minh City is a big mouthful," he replies, grinning.

At the hotel, General Chi excuses himself: he is staying with one of his daughters who lives in the city, and he has promised to be home early tonight. But Mr. Giai and Luu agree to have dinner with us. We go to the My Canh—meaning Beautiful Scene—floating restaurant on the river close to the hotel.

Barely five feet tall, with thin gray hair and thick glasses, Mr. Giai is turning out to be a sprightly and good-humored man. He tells us of the one time in his life when he actually met Ho Chi Minh. It was in Hanoi, near the end of Ho's life. "I was trying to take his picture," he says, "and other people kept getting in the way. He shooed the other people away, and said to me, 'If you're going to do something, do it right.' He said that to me. And then he shook my hand. And I got a good picture, too."

He tells us he is the father of eight children. He joined the Viet Minh in 1945, eventually achieved the rank of captain, and served under General Chi. He was wounded three times—he holds up his hand with the missing thumb: once by the French and twice by the Americans. His oldest son was killed by American soldiers in the Central Highlands in 1965.

Born in Hanoi in 1956, Luu was too young to have fought in the war. Like Miss Loan, he was evacuated from the city when the American bombing began, and he remembers the raids vividly. Once, he tells us, he saw a captured American pilot being marched through the streets. The people were so angry, he says, that they tried to beat the pilot, and the soldiers had to protect him.

"You must miss your wife," Mr. Giai says, turning to me.

"I do," I laugh. "Three weeks seems like an eternity. I've seldom been away from her overnight in the five years we've been married."

"Once, during the French war," he says, "I was separated from my wife for nine years." There is no hint of irony or condescension in his voice. He is simply commiserating with me.

"It must seem a little dull these days," I say, "after all those years of soldiering." He stares at me with a puzzled look. "You know, as awful as war is," I try to explain, "after all you've seen and done, doesn't it seem dull sometimes to live such a quiet life?"

"Oh, no," he replies quickly, "I did what was necessary, but I never liked it. Give me a hundred years of peace. A thousand years. I don't want any more war."

Later, as we walk back to the hotel, Mr. Giai takes my hand in his as if I were his grandson. Such a curious and beautiful custom, this business of holding hands. Men and women, of course, seldom hold hands in public; it would be scandalous, a breach of social etiquette. But two men, or two women — then it is only a sign of friendship and affection.

The last time I was in Vietnam, we used to think that two men holding hands must be homosexuals. We were convinced that half the men in Vietnam were "queer." And we let them know it, often and rudely. No one — from the president of the United States on down — ever bothered to tell us what holding hands meant. I doubt that they even knew.

Later, I go for a walk alone. "Jimmy," the Amerasian cyclo driver, follows me up the street, along with half a dozen other drivers. One says, "You're an American, aren't you?" His pronunciation is so clear and distinct that I stop and turn toward him. "Communism stinks," he spits out.

"Watch out for the cyclo drivers," John's old friend had warned, "They're all secret police." This guy is the secret police? If he is, I think, he's a hell of a good actor.

"Where did you learn to speak English?" I ask him. He explains that he had been a Vietnamese Marine for seven years and had learned English then, working as an interpreter with various American units. He describes the area around Da Nang accurately, and even mentions a number of American units by name. After the war, he says, he was put into a re-education camp for four years. What rank was he, I ask. A corporal, he replies.

"Why did they keep you in the camps for so long?" I ask.

"Because I was a translator," he replies, "They thought I knew more than I did. We can't talk here. Ride with me."

But I don't want to ride. There is nothing I can do for this man. "Not tonight," I tell him, and turn away.

"Maybe tomorrow you will ride with me," he calls after me.

In the park across from the old National Assembly, I spot the "Sugar Cane Kid," the same boy I had seen yesterday. He offers me a seat beside him on a bench. It is hard to communicate, but I manage — I think — to gather that he is nine years old and lives in Cholon. We are soon joined by a girl who looks vaguely Amerasian, as though she might be one-quarter French, perhaps. Her name is Lan, she says, and she is 14, though she looks much younger. Both children are polite and give a sense of quiet self-assurance. Both seem clean and cared for. What are they doing out on the street at 9 p.m., I wonder. Do they go to school, I ask. Both say that they do. Where does Lan live, I ask. "Far away," she indicates, pointing. In the city? Yes, she says.

But I'm not at all sure they understand my questions, or I their answers. We sit for awhile longer, playing hand games and making faces. They seem to find me very amusing. Neither child asks me for anything. I buy them each a popsicle from a street vendor. They snuggle up on either side of me, smiling up at me as they lick their sticky treats.

Friday, December 27

The People's Fatherland Front is a social and political umbrella group, we are told, made up of representatives of a wide range of groups: women, peasants, religious, ethnic minorities, youth, trade, "patriotic bourgeoisie" and the Party. Front Vice President Pham Van Ba explains that the Front does not get involved with questions of ideology, but serves as a kind of advisory board on policies for rebuilding Vietnam. Its purposes, he says, are to unite the country for defense and reconstruction, and to build international solidarity.

The group gathered this morning is daunting merely by virtue of its size: a writer, a lawyer, a former Saigon general, the general secretary of the Ho Chi Minh Friendship Committee, a businessman, a former vice minister for foreign affairs in the old Provisional Revolutionary Government, a former Saigon lieutenant who is now vice director of a hospital, an ethnic Cambodian, a former member of the old Saigon national assembly, a Buddhist monk, a Catholic priest, a professor and an oceanographer. I could spend half a day talking to each person, but we have only one morning for all of them. Do we have any questions, we are asked.

Bruce asks if the northern leadership—the old DRV, what used to be called North Vietnam—betrayed the southern NLF/PRG after the end of the war. It is the charge made by former PRG Justice Minister Tang. No, the former PRG member replies, there could be no such "betrayal" because the struggle had always been "a struggle of all the people, north and south." During the Paris peace talks, he explains, Nguyen Van Thieu demanded that all North Vietnamese Army troops be withdrawn from the south, but both the DRV and the NLF/PRG rejected this demand because NVA troops could not be considered "invaders" since Vietnam was all one country. That the U.S. agreed to allow NVA troops to remain in the south as part of the treaty, he argues, demonstrated American acceptance of this fact. Furthermore, he says, rapid reunification had always been the goal of all the revolutionary forces, and many members of the old NLF/PRG now hold important positions in the new unified government. The strategy of foreign aggressors, he reminds us, has always been to divide Vietnam, but the Vietnamese have always resisted division.

Is religion tolerated under the new regime, John asks. There is no strife between Buddhists and Catholics on the one hand and the government on the other hand, says the Buddhist venerable. "The light is for all people," he says, somewhat enigmatically and without further explanation. The Catholic priest says nothing.

Are people better off now economically, I ask. Largely because of the loss of foreign aid and the collapse of the false war economy, the businessman replies, the standard of living in the cities has declined, but rural life is better because of the absence of war. Also, there is less difference between the highest and lowest incomes. There are still differences in income, he says, but not nearly so much as in former times, and things are improving.

"Things will be better," adds the former Saigon general, "if not for us, then for our children and grandchildren. First we must establish a foundation we can build on, and we must learn better management skills."

The former general, whose name is Nguyen Huu Hanh, is one of the highest ranking former Saigon officers still in Vietnam. He had fought with the French against the Viet Minh, and later studied military science during two tours of duty in the United States. Later in the war, he had been deputy commander of both Military Region II and Military Region IV. Staunchly anticommunist, he had spent 29 years in the old Saigon army, and one of his sons had been killed fighting the communists.

General Hanh had been an ally and protégé of Duong Van Minh. Minh had played a major role in the overthrow of Diem and had taken control of the government only to be overthrown himself three months later in January 1964. Over eleven years later, in the last days of the old regime, after Thieu had fled with his millions in gold, Minh had become the last president of the southern Republic of Vietnam. He had appointed Hanh deputy chief of staff of the armed forces, and it was General Hanh who gave the order to the Army of the Republic of Vietnam to lay down their arms and surrender — an order that undoubtedly saved countless thousands of lives.

Was he angered by the sudden curtailment of American aid in the last months of the war, we ask. "No," he says, "it helped us to resolve the war quickly." He repeats the charge that China offered aid to the Thieu regime to continue the war. Does he think the United States was behind this offer, we ask. "I don't know," he replies. "It is plausible."

Was he sent to a re-education camp, we ask. Only for a brief time, he replies.

Why did he stay behind, we ask. "I am not a communist," he replies, "but I was misinformed about communism. This is my country, and the important thing is to rebuild it. After World War Two, we thought the Americans would help us gain independence; instead, United States military and civilian advisors decided everything." The cost of the war became too high, he says, and finally his first priority became to stop the war; then the Vietnamese could decide for themselves what government they should have. "My hope is that eventually the Vietnamese will adapt the Soviet model to suit Vietnamese realities."

General Chi realizes that the group is much too large and unwieldy. He suggests that we break into smaller groups, so that John, Bruce and I can engage more of the people who have taken their time to be here. I end up in a discussion with Dr. Bui Thi Lang, an oceanographer, who tells me that she studied at the Scripps Institute in La Jolla, California. Now she is involved in environmental restoration of the coastlines, especially the mangrove swamps.

Did she work for the revolution during the war, I ask Dr. Lang. No, she replies, she has always been nonpolitical, a teacher and a scientist. But occasionally, she explains, she was able to help out students of hers who got into trouble with the old regime. Now she finds that some of her former students hold positions of power, and she is often able to help out friends who get into trouble with the new regime. "I just do what I can," she says, "That's all I've ever done."

She asks if we've had "any trouble" during our visit. What does she mean, I ask. She explains that a year or two earlier, she took a trip to Ca Mau in the Mekong Delta with a visiting American scientist. "When the people saw him," she says, "the women began screaming and crying. Some people tried to shoot him." No, I reply, more than a little startled, no one has tried to shoot me yet. She explains that hatred of Americans is much stronger in the rural areas than it is in the cities. "The cities did not suffer the way the countryside did," she says.

"So much was destroyed during the war," she continues, "and we are short of scientific equipment, good information and funds. If only we had better relations with the United States. There is so much we could do with a little help." She explains that Dr. Ed Cooperman, a physicist at the University of Southern California, had been sending her scientific journals, but now he is dead.

I have heard of Cooperman. A vocal advocate of normal relations between the United States and Vietnam, he had been shot to death by a Vietnamese refugee perhaps eighteen months earlier. There had been—and there remains—deep suspicion that Cooperman had been targeted for execution by the right-wing refugee community, but during the trial it was ruled that the assassin had acted independently. He was convicted only of manslaughter and will be eligible for parole as early as 1987.

Dr. Lang tells me that since Cooperman's death, she has been afraid to ask any other American scientist to send her materials. She says she would like to come to the United States herself to gather information and renew old ties with professional colleagues, but she fears that right-wing Vietnamese refugees might try to kill her, too. "My brother was in the Saigon air force," she says; "I know Nguyen Cao Ky"—who was air vice marshal, as well as premier and vice president—"I know what he is like."

In the afternoon, we go to the New Youth Labor Training Center, a rehabilitation center for drug addicts. We are received by the center's director, Nguyen Quang Van, in a building with colored glass windows and a stone cross on its roof. It must have been a church at one time, but inside now is a large flag of the Socialist Republic of Vietnam, and a bust of Ho Chi Minh on a high pedestal flanked by portraits of Lenin and Marx.

Mr. Van, who says he was a VC military cadre in Saigon during the war, explains that there were 100,000 addicts in Saigon alone by the end of the war. Sixteen thousand people have graduated from this center since 1975, and there are 800 addicts here now, ranging in age from 20 to 70. About 10 percent are women. Patients—he calls them "pupils"—arrive in one of three ways: some come in voluntarily, others are committed by their families, while about 70 percent are brought in after being arrested on drug-related charges.

The first part of the treatment, he explains, is detoxification. It is done "cold turkey." To ease the pain of withdrawal, five methods are used: acupuncture, massage, warm water baths, gymnastics and traditional herbs. Depending on the patient, this phase takes one week to one month.

The second part of the treatment consists of psychological education. Pupils lack belief in themselves, he says, so the center tries to instill self-confidence, teaching love, conscience, the value of labor, and rejection of drug dealers and smugglers. An important element is the reestablishing of loving ties with the pupils' families. This phase lasts about three months.

Finally, he says, pupils are given vocational training in agriculture and handicrafts. The products are sold and the proceeds divided among the center and the pupils. Food and medicine are provided by the state, but all other funds needed to run the center—including staff salaries—are provided through the sale of the pupils' products. In 1985, he says, the center sold 40 million dong worth of goods. Staff salaries range from 260 to 400 dong a month. "A good student worker," he says, "can earn more money than the staff members."

Pupils are confined to the school for the first six months, he explains, then they can go out occasionally, but they are always followed to make sure they don't revert to their old ways. Though availability of drugs is far less widespread than it had been in former times, he explains, drugs can still be had. Heroin used to be the major problem, but now it is opium. We ask about marijuana. Yes, he says, it's available, but it's not considered a serious problem.

Drug addiction is difficult to break, he says. Soon after they arrive, up to 90 percent of the pupils don't want to stay. Attempted suicides are a problem, as are self-inflicted wounds which require hospitalization, offering an easier chance of escape. Still, he says, there are no police at the school; discipline and oversight are entirely self-managed by the staff and the pupils.

He takes us on a tour of the center. We watch an older man receiving acupuncture treatment, a group of men doing calisthenics, and other pupils making shoes, carpets, various kinds of furniture, and spare parts for bicycles and motorscooters. In one room is a display of beautiful wooden cabinets and guitars, all made by pupils and all for sale. In another room is a small drug museum. On one wall is a chart indicating the involvement in drug trafficking of the old Saigon regime.

According to the chart, Diem's brother Ngo Dinh Nhu had headed the list of smugglers until his assassination during the November 1963 coup. After Diem's overthrow, the major figures at the top of the chart are Nguyen Cao Ky, Nguyen Van Thieu, Nguyen Ngoc Loan and Tran Thien Khiem. The chart also alleges that the CIA was linked to the Saigon heroin trade, an allegation that has been suggested by numerous sources in the United States, including Alfred W. McCoy in his 1972 book, *The Politics of Heroin in Southeast Asia*. Essentially, the allegation is that heroin was knowingly flown from the Golden Triangle of Burma-Thailand-Laos to Saigon at the behest of the Saigon generals aboard Air America planes. The CIA and the Saigon generals, not surprisingly, have always denied these charges.

On the way back into town, John asks if he can be dropped off at the old Saigon Botanical Gardens, and I decide to go with him. What we find is a shabby affair that must once have been very beautiful. The gardens themselves seem not to have gotten much attention recently, perhaps not since the end of the war, and the few remaining caged animals—cats, primates and birds—are surrounded by their own filth. Given the terrible economic burden of the country, it is not surprising to see a park neglected, but the deplorable state of these once-wild beasts is as heartbreaking as anything I've seen so far. As we walk by one of the food kiosks, a tape recorder is playing in English: "Listen to the Rhythm of the Falling Rain," a popular American ballad of the early 1960s.

"Do you remember my poem 'On Opening Le Ba Khon's Dictionary'?" John asks as we stand looking over an iron fence down into the bear pits. Indeed, I remember John's poem well:

> *So the Soul, that Drop, that Ray*
> *of the clear Fountain of Eternal Day,*
> *Could it within the humane flow'r be seen.*
> — Andrew Marvell, "On a Drop of Dew"

The ink-specked sheets feel like cigar leaf;
its crackling spine flutters up a mildewed must.
Unlike the lacquered box which dry-warp detonated
—shattering pearled poet, moon, and willow pond—
the book survived, but begs us both go back
to the Bibliotheque in the Musee at the Jardin in Saigon,
where I would lean from ledges of high windows
to see the zoo's pond, isled with Chinese pavilion,
arched bridge where kids fed popcorn to gulping carp,
and shaded benches, where whores fanned their make-up,
at ease because a man who feeds the peacocks
can't be that much of a beast. A boatride,
a soda, a stroll through the flower beds.
On weekends the crowds could forget the war.

At night police tortured men in the bear pits,
one night a man held out the bag of his own guts,
which streamed and weighed in his open hands,
and offered them to a bear. Nearby, that night
the moon was caught in willows by the pond,
shone scattered in droplets on the flat lotus pads,
each bead bright like the dew in Marvell's rose.

"This is where the Saigon police used to interrogate prisoners," says John, "Down there, with the bears." Below us, two restless bears pace the concrete, now and then rearing up on their hind legs, pawing the air.

Walking from the gardens to the hotel, I notice there are few cyclo drivers and no beggars—children or otherwise. In this part of the city, I feel as comfortable as I did in Hanoi. It is the *first* time I've felt at ease out walking since we've come south. I mention it to John.

"They all hang around the downtown hotels," John conjectures, "That's where the Westerners stay. That's where the money is. It's sad. As soon as they find out you're an American . . . some of them still think the Americans can save them."

We pass a large Catholic cathedral complex just as school is being let out for the day. Children, all of them girls, rush out into the street, laughing and running and shouting. Intent upon freedom after being cooped up in class all afternoon, most of them don't even seem to notice us. Down by the river, we pass the gate of a Vietnamese navy base. Three young sailors on guard duty wave at us and smile.

Walking alone up to the square after supper, I encounter a boy I have seen every time I've walked this way. He is impossible to miss. He has a hip deformity, and walks on all fours, his rear end high in the air, his head down low. He begs money with particular urgency and openness, following along, tugging at my clothing. I have seen other children taunting him on several occasions.

Lan is not in the square tonight, but the Sugar Cane Kid is. So are several other children. One of them is black Amerasian. He seems to be accepted by the other kids, but how can I know? All of them seem on their best behavior in the presence of this strange foreigner, though a few of them quietly ask for money or shampoo. The black Amerasian asks for nothing. He picks up a discarded cigarette pack, removes the foil lining and flattens it out carefully, then proceeds to fashion an intricate silver flower out of it. When I get up to leave, he gives me the flower, twisting the stem through the upper buttonhole of my jacket.

Cu Chi District

We have the same car today that we had yesterday—the first time we've had the same car two days in a row since we came south—and the same driver. From the small sampling we've had since we've been in Vietnam, it appears that Vietnamese drivers do not believe in downshifting. The car goes into second gear at 10 miles per hour, into third gear at 15, and thereafter—come hell or high water, ox-carts or slow-moving buses—it becomes a matter of principle not to downshift. Our present driver is so adept at not downshifting that we've taken to calling him "Downshift Charlie." In a country woefully short on spare parts, laboring the engine so constantly and so badly seems a curious way to treat a precious commodity.

As we drive along the road to Cu Chi in the early morning light, General Chi asks us if we know any good jokes. Bruce tells the one about the elephant who encountered the naked man. The elephant points to the man's "trunk" and asks: "How can you drink with that thing?" The general howls with laughter. John tries the one about the lion, the monkey and the *New York Times*, but it is a long complicated joke and apparently loses something in translation. General Chi laughs politely, Luu shrugs his shoulders, and we give up on jokes in favor of asking the general more about his own life.

He explains that he was a young lieutenant colonel at the battle of Dien Bien Phu. To reach the battlefield, he had had to walk over 800 kilometers. After the garrison's surrender, he was assigned to escort the French commander, Colonel Christian de Castries, back to Hanoi. "It was a difficult journey," he says, "de Castries was very sick, and I had to give him all of my own medicine. If he had died along the way," he laughs, "it would have been my backside."

Had the French not given up after Dien Bien Phu, we ask, could the Viet Minh have continued fighting? I have heard, I tell him, that it was

China and the Soviet Union that pressured Ho Chi Minh into accepting the Geneva settlement of 1954, which called for reunification elections by 1956 — elections which never took place because Diem and his American backers refused to participate, necessitating another 21 years of war.

The 1954 settlement was not entirely China's fault, the general replies. After nine years of war, the Viet Minh needed a rest. "Besides," the general adds, "why fight when you can have an election?" And Ho fully expected to win that election, and almost assuredly would have, had it been held — a prospect in which United States intelligence sources at the time concurred, though the American people did not learn this until *The Pentagon Papers* were released.

Still, he says, if China had supported it, the division of the country could have been made further south, at the 14th or 15th parallel instead of at the 17th. At that time, however, Vietnam thought China was its friend and did not recognize China's lack of support for the betrayal that it was. He makes no mention of the Soviet Union's acquiesence in the division at the 17th parallel.

The car sputters to a stop, and we all get out to stretch our legs as the driver begins tinkering under the hood. What will happen to Vietnam if Soviet-Chinese relations improve, we ask. In recent months, there has been a noticeable thawing in Sino-Soviet relations for the first time in twenty years. Does it worry the general? No, he replies, the Soviets have assured Vietnam that better Soviet relations with either China or the United States will not jeopardize Vietnamese interests.

Downshift Charlie seems to be a better mechanic than he is a driver. The car has succumbed to a blocked fuel pump, but he has managed to fix it by using parts from a bicycle pump provided by a passing peasant. We take off again and soon arrive at the headquarters of the People's Committee for Cu Chi District.

Throughout the war, Cu Chi was a major VC stronghold. Located 35 kilometers west of Ho Chi Minh City, it was recognized by all sides as "the gateway to Saigon." Consequently, it was a free fire zone that was virtually leveled during the war. Dao Van Duc, vice president of the People's Committee, tells us that there were three major U.S./ARVN bases within the district, 200 smaller outposts, and many strategic hamlets throughout.

"The U.S. and the puppets failed to sever relations between the fighters and the people, however," he says, adding that out of 80,000 total inhabitants in the district, 16,000 were in the liberation army, and thousands of others provided support in other ways. Ten thousand families lost family members, and the district produced 18 "state heroes" — their equivalent of winners of the Congressional Medal of Honor.

After coffee, tea and fruit, we go to "Traditional House," the district museum, built just last spring for the tenth anniversary of the end of the war. Here we see a film about the war in Cu Chi and the process of reconstruction after the war. We learn that the district produces rice, soy beans, peanuts, sugar cane, tobacco and corn, that 10,000 hectares of land have been reclaimed since the end of the war, bringing the district's total of land under cultivation to 32,000 hectares, that in ten years' time over 500 people have been killed accidentally by unexploded mines and dud rounds including, most recently, an old man and three children. Mr. Duc shows us a display case filled with new farm implements, explaining that the tools were made from salvaged metal at a factory that used to produce explosives.

Then he shows us a large wall map of the district with a series of color-coded lights imbedded in it. It reminds me of the civil war battle map I saw as a child on display at Gettysburg, Pennsylvania. The yellow lights are ARVN bases, Mr. Duc explains, the red lights are U.S. bases, and the green lights are VC bases. There were four major VC bases in Cu Chi. One of them was only two kilometers from the largest ARVN base, he says, pointing to the map, but none of them was ever discovered.

From the museum, we drive to the district hospital. There are 10 doctors and 100 beds, but a new wing now under construction will add another 50 beds. In addition to the hospital, he says proudly, "every village in the district now has a clinic."

From the hospital, we go to the Cu Chi Orphanage. Immediately after the war, he tells us, there were 600 orphans here, but only 200 remain, all ranging in age from 15 to 17, the others having graduated already. We watch a group of young men and women operating ancient looms driven by electricity. All of the children, he says, are given training in agriculture or one of several vocations. The grounds are largely barren, the buildings stark and unadorned, the architecture suggesting that the orphanage might once have been an ARVN base. Funds to help the orphanage have been promised from UNESCO, he says, but they haven't arrived yet.

Back at the district headquarters, we eat a lunch of freshly baked bread, a kind of lunch meat, cold roast chicken, vegetable rice soup, and lettuce and tomato salad. "We are entirely economically self-sufficient," says Mr. Duc, explaining that everything on the table comes from within the district. He offers us each a pack of Bong Hong cigarettes, made in a local factory from locally grown tobacco. Bong Hong means "Rose." I know this because, while the front of the pack is printed in Vietnamese, the back is printed in English.

"Did Mr. Duc tell you that he has three degrees?" General Chi asks us, smiling. He puts his arm around Mr. Giai. "The younger generation is wiser than we are. Between the two of us, we don't even have a high school diploma."

"When you two were young," Mr. Duc replies quickly, "there were more important things to do than go to school."

"There weren't any schools," says Mr. Giai.

After lunch, we drive to Pham Van Coi state farm. "All of this used to be an American base," says Mr. Duc as we stand by the edge of a vast sugar cane field, but there is no evidence at all that the Americans had ever been here. It is almost eerie, but strangely satisfying.

There are three types of collectivized farming, Mr. Duc explains. The least organized is the mutual production group. Ownership of tools and land is private and production decisions are made by each farmer, but labor is often pooled, as is the money to buy things like fertilizer in quantity. Eventually, several production groups might evolve into a cooperative, the second type of collectivized agriculture. The cooperative governs itself, determining how to allocate land and tools and what to do with profits. Cooperative members, however, are permitted small family plots for animal husbandry and private gardens. The third type is the state farm, which represents a kind of capital investment by the government. The land belongs to the state, and workers are paid fixed salaries just as if they worked in a factory.

Do cooperatives eventually evolve into state farms, we ask. No, he replies, they are two different entities entirely, serving different needs and functions. There are five state farms in Cu Chi and 98 cooperatives. Are people forced to join collectives of one sort or another, we ask. "After liberation," he replies, "we tried to collectivize too rapidly, but people weren't ready for it and the policy was a failure. Now we try to encourage people to join by example. We hope that when people see their neighbors prospering, they too will want to join."

A small crowd of people has gradually accumulated around us as we stand talking — pedestrian and bike traffic, attracted by the foreigners. One of them is an older man who hails Mr. Duc by name. Strapped to his bicycle is a green metal cyclinder. "It's part of an American rocket," the man explains when I point to the U.S. markings stamped into the metal. "I made it into a water pump." Then he grins broadly. "I like it better as a water pump," he laughs. "It's a very good water pump."

We stop again along another road, but here the landscape looks more like the moon. There are large craters everywhere, laid out as if in deliberate rows. Some of them are full of stagnant water. The earth around them is rock-hard and barren of life, except for a few scrubby weeds. "B-52s," Mr. Duc says, though I don't need to be told. I've seen the results of B-52 strikes before, up on the DMZ back in 1967. And though this site is old and eroded, I recognize the systematic pattern of the craters. "We're filling in the craters as fast as we can," Mr. Duc says, almost apologetically, "But we have to haul earth from a long distance, and we have very little heavy equipment, so it all has to be done with manual labor."

As we stand looking at the craters, an enclosed two-wheeled cart comes down the road drawn by a small pony. I don't recall ever having seen ponies farther north during the war. The cart is gaily painted, and the pony wears a bell collar and a bristled headdress that bobs and tosses as the pony trots by. The whole rig looks like something I'd more expect to see in the Carpathian mountains than here on the coastal plain of Vietnam.

Later, as we inspect a new cement-lined irrigation canal, Mr. Duc explains that most of the district has been electrified since the end of the war. Nearby, a farmer plows a field behind a team of oxen while several barrel-bodied gray water buffalo graze not far away, their heavy curved horns tossing as their heads move from side to side. Brick kilns are everywhere to be seen, together with many new brick houses, obviously the final products of the kilns. The fields are dry and brown, the rice ripe, and the harvest season in full swing. Along the shoulders of every road, and even on the road surfaces themselves, rice husks dry on straw mats beneath a scorching midday sun.

All day long I have been feeling an oddly satisfying sense of *déjà vu* for the first time since I've been here, and as I stand looking all around me I suddenly understand why. This is the first time we've gotten out of the cities. Everywhere I look are houses standing alone amid green trees or clustered together in small groups, buffalo in the fields—some with children on their backs—men and women laboriously threshing rice by hand, graceful fishing nets perched on long bamboo poles above small waterways. This is the Vietnam I remember: rural, simple, almost eternal.

What's different is the absence of war, the absence of Americans and barbed wire and artillery, the whop-whop of chopperblades and the whine of jet fighters. Gone are the shacks made of discarded tin and C-ration cardboard, replaced by brick houses with tile roofs. Gone are the crump of exploding mortars and the heavy clanking of tanks, replaced by the steady padding of bare feet carrying rice to the threshers and the swish of rice stalks striking the threshing mats.

This is what I came here for. Half my life I have longed to witness peace in this land I have never been able to see in my mind's eye except in the midst of war. So what if it's Cu Chi instead of Hieu Nhon? Look at it, boy, I think to myself, take it all in. Remember this. It is harvest time, and the threshing floors are dancing with rice. There are winners and there are losers, but the war is over.

Then Mr. Duc takes us to visit Mrs. Na, who lost all five of her sons in the war. "You did this to me," she says, and it all comes flooding back. But Mrs. Na's sons weren't exactly innocent bystanders, I try to remind myself as I stare down at the bare table, they were Viet Cong guerrillas. Fighters. And what would I have been, had I been one of Mrs. Na's sons? I know what I would have been, and I don't know what to say to Mrs. Na. I feel nauseated — truly ill. I don't want to be here.

Mr. Duc explains that we are friends, that we have come in peace — though he does not tell her that Bruce and I are former soldiers. "Okay," she nods, "if you say so." But she hardly seems convinced. I think of the story Dr. Lang told me just yesterday about the American scientist at Ca Mau, and my stomach wrenches violently. It is all I can do to keep from bolting out the door.

Finally, after what seems like forever, we get up to leave. At the door, I take Mrs. Na's hand in both of mine and force myself to look her in the face. "I'm sorry about your sons," I tell her. "I'm sorry about the war."

As we walk back to the car, Luu slips his arm firmly around my waist, as if trying to steady me. "That was hard for you, wasn't it?" he says. I wonder if I look as sick as I feel.

"Yes," I reply, grateful and touched by his sensitivity.

By the time we arrive at the open pavilion commemorating the tunnels of Cu Chi, the nausea has receded and I'm feeling a little better. We are greeted by Tran Thi Bich, who embraces General Chi with a warm hug — a public display of affection between the sexes permissible only because the general is old enough to be Miss Bich's father — and the general is clearly delighted with the attention.

The tunnels of Cu Chi are famous. The first tunnels were built back in 1948, Mr. Duc explains, and by 1965 the VC had constructed over 320 kilometers of interconnecting honeycombs, ingeniously camouflaged and murderously boobytrapped. The Americans knew the tunnels existed, but were never able to locate more than a small portion of them, and never knew just how extensive the system was. Because of the constant bombing and military operations in Cu Chi, Mr. Duc explains, life above ground became impossible. Every conceivable activity was carried on in the tunnels: schools, hospitals, munitions factories, kitchens, even cinemas—the entire district simply moved underground. Some of the tunnels even went right under American installations.

"Sometimes we would scurry out of the tunnels inside your lines, plant mines on the helicopters, and run back into the tunnels without being detected," says Miss Bich, giggling almost playfully. Now 28, Miss Bich grew up in the tunnels, she tells us, from age 8 to age 18. She herself mostly served as a courier, transmitting messages from one post to another or gathering visual intelligence.

A small portion of the tunnels is still kept open as a kind of living museum, and General Chi insists that we go down. I'm not too keen on the idea, but he doesn't leave much room for debate, pointing to the hole and nodding. It is hot, dark and close inside, the tunnel twisting and turning, rising and descending, pitch black and horribly confining. I'm frightened, but Miss Bich keeps urging us forward. I follow the sound of her voice, desperately searching for the light at the end of the tunnel, groping along on hands and knees, my head scraping the ceiling, my shoulders brushing the sides. How could people actually live down here year in and year out, I wonder, let alone wage war so effectively? No wonder they beat us.

Finally I reach the end and climb out through a narrow trapdoor. I'm sweating heavily, breathing hard, and quite chagrined to discover that we've traveled all of 50 meters. Miss Bich reaches down to offer me a hand up. Her red Communist Youth League pin catches the sun as she smiles and takes my hand.

We stop later at Thuan Phong hamlet to wash the tunnel dust from our throats, and Mr. Duc treats us each to a glass of orangeade made from orange pulp and sugar mixed with water right in the glass. There is even ice. I am dying of thirst, but worried about drinking the water. I have no idea whether or not it has been boiled. I wonder if I should ask Mr. Duc, but everyone else is drinking it, including John and Bruce, and I am too embarrassed to ask. I'm also very thirsty. I drink the orangeade and hope for the best. As we drink and cool off, Mr. Duc explains that

Thuan Phong has been built since the war on a site once bulldozed flat by the Americans. The hamlet is now the focal point for the whole village, containing the clinic and a brand-new 3,500-seat outdoor theater.

We walk from the "soda shop" to a small river where we can see the rotting ribs of what had once been a boat perhaps 40 feet long. The remains are resting on land, only a few meters from the river's edge, and Mr. Duc says that the boat had once been a ferry, but in 1964, "puppet troops" sank it with rockets. Two hundred people were killed, he says.

Several water buffalo and oxen are tethered in the fields nearby, and a few small children turn to watch the foreigners. As Mr. Duc talks, two men wade waist-deep in the river, tugging behind them a small boat loaded with bags of rice. A woman unloads rice from another boat tied to the riverbank, patiently filling two baskets at a time, carrying them on a long pole slung across her shoulders to a nearby house, then returning to the boat to refill the baskets still another time. She makes several trips while we are there, and she is still at it as we leave. If she has noticed us, she has given no indication of it. She has work to do. Life goes on.

Sunday, December 29

After the long day in Cu Chi, today's schedule is very light: only one meeting in the afternoon. We sleep in, then go shopping at the big market on the far side of Nguyen Hue Boulevard. Bruce and John need shampoo. I want to buy some silk for Anne.

Unlike the Cholon Market and the markets of Old Hanoi, this one is completely enclosed in a one-story building. Inside, it is so crowded that it is almost impossible to move, and the temperature is easily 20 degrees hotter than it is on the street. I feel like I'm stuck in a Philadelphia street car at rush hour in August.

The variety of manufactured goods is much larger than it was in Hanoi. I notice products from Japan, Australia, Singapore and a number of Eastern and Western European countries, as well as Vietnamese goods—everything from toothpaste and shampoo to Sanyo radios and Sony tape recorders.

We have problems buying shampoo, however. We have no small change, and neither does the cashier. Making change has been a constant problem ever since we arrived in Hanoi. No one seems to have any small bills—all money being made of paper these days, perhaps reflecting the shortage of metal. Sometimes the hotel desk has change, but you have to get there just as the hotel restaurant's receipts are being tallied for the day. We even tried to get change from the bank once, but we were told that none was available.

At last another customer is able to help us out, and we buy the shampoo and leave. All three of us are about ready to pass out from the heat and claustrophobia. I will look for silk in one of the silk shops along Dong Khoi Street; even though I will probably end up paying more, it is better than dying of suffocation in the market.

At the Khanh Ngoc Silk Shop, I find a piece of deep green silk lavishly hand-embroidered with pale green, white and yellow flowers.

Two square yards, it sells for 650 dong. At the black market exchange rate, it would go for $6.50. But even at the official exchange rate—the hotel is giving 18 dong to the dollar, slightly better than the rate in Hanoi—this magnificent piece of cloth costs me only $36.10.

Further down the street, in a government-owned store, I buy a cassette tape of traditional Vietnamese music for $2, which I must pay for in dollars. Because of past encounters with "traditional" music, I ask the clerk to play part of the tape first before I hand over the money.

Across the street is a barbershop. I don't need a haircut, but I notice they are also giving scalp massages, too, so I decide to get one of those. The shop manager—owner, perhaps?—is an older man, but all four of the barbers are women in their 30s or early 40s. One of them motions me to her chair. As she begins to work, she asks me if I am an American. Then she tells me she used to work for the Americans as a secretary.

Stopping frequently and speaking quietly, she tells me that on the last day of the war, she tried to get out. She took her two children to the American embassy, but there was so much shooting that she had to huddle in a gutter all day. When night came she went home. "My brother got out," she says. "He's a doctor now for the U.S. Veterans Administration in St. Cloud, Minnesota."

One part of me truly aches with sympathy for her, but another part of me wants to shout: "What do you expect me to do about it, lady?" These one-sided exchanges have begun to exact their toll. I have long believed that my government abandoned those it should not have abandoned and saved those it should not have saved. But I cannot change the past. What do these people expect me to do, I wonder, stuff them in my suitcase and whisk them away with me? Perhaps it is as John says, that even after ten long years, many of these people still retain a mystical sense of the power of Americans, that somehow the Americans will yet miraculously save them from their misery.

Go talk to Mrs. Na, I want to tell the barber; talk to Miss Tao or Miss Bich. For every one of you there is one of them. Had your side won—my side—I strongly suspect such people would have died long ago at the hands of men capable of interrogating suspects in a bear pit and selling heroin to the soldiers of their own allies. This is your country and no one is going to save you, and the sooner you understand that, the better off you will be.

I do not want to become hard-hearted. I don't think I am a fool. What is happening in this country is not some socialist utopia. I have often wondered whatever became of my ARVN friend, Staff Sergeant

Suong, who could quote Baudelaire in French and who had the heart of a lion. But even Suong had finally reached his limit, quitting one hot day in September 1967, shouting, "You Americans come here with your tanks and your jets and your helicopters, and everywhere you go, the VC grow like new rice in the fields. You are worse than the Viet Cong." Would he still feel that way, 18 years later?

I will never know. Nor will I ever know what might have happened had Woodrow Wilson deigned to give Ho Chi Minh an audience back in 1919, had Harry Truman heeded the recommendations of Archimedes Patti in 1945, had Dwight Eisenhower supported reunification elections in 1954, had Lyndon Johnson declined to send in the Marines in 1965. So many potential turning points. So many lost opportunities. To look at the war as if it began on April 29, 1975 — to say that if we had only fought longer, harder, sent more troops, dropped more bombs, jailed the hippies and antiwar protesters — is to ignore the consistent failure and utter bankruptcy of thirty years of American foreign policy in Southeast Asia. Vietnam was never ours to dispose of.

I thank the woman for the massage, give her a tip, and leave. Out on the street, I spot the black Amerasian I met two nights ago in the square, and I wave to him. He is walking with a white Amerasian girl. He approaches me, but she hangs back. We walk together to the hotel, the boy and I side by side, the girl following a few feet behind. "I have to go now," I tell him. "Maybe I see you tonight." He points back up the street toward the square, smiles, then waves goodbye. I wink at the girl and she breaks into a radiant smile, a single dimple suddenly appearing on her left cheek.

Mr. Anh is the vice director of the SINCO Sewing Machine Factory. Mr. Hiu is the factory's chief planner. The factory produces old-style, pedal-powered sewing machines, heavier industrial sewing machines, and adding machines. The machines used to be assembled from parts imported from Hong Kong and Japan, the two men tell us, but since 1979 they have been wholly manufactured in Vietnam. The factory currently produces 6,000 machines per year, a figure less than the factory's potential capacity due to a shortage of raw materials. To maximize capacity, it has recently begun producing children's furniture and toys.

Can workers strike if conditions are not good, we ask. There is no need to strike, they reply; the workers control the factory; if there are problems, they are settled by discussion. Factory management and trade union representatives elected by the workers jointly determine work plans and production quotas.

How much are workers paid, we ask. The minimum wage is 290 a month, they reply, but with bonuses included, a good worker can bring home as much as 600 to 800 dong.

Can workers be fired? Yes, of course, they reply, but only as a last resort. "The majority of workers realize their responsibilities," says Mr. Anh.

General Chi tells us that many of the factory's workers are former members of the old regime. That's right, says Mr. Anh, explaining that both he and Mr. Hiu were ARVN lieutenants. Are such people discriminated against, we ask.

Mr. Hiu replies that he had been afraid of discrimination when he went to work at the factory in 1978, but that it never materialized. "They only care how well you work," he says.

"I'm vice director of the factory," Mr. Anh adds. "I'm responsible for 300 workers. What more can I say?"

"But you fought against the communists," I reply. "How do you explain the transformation?"

Mr. Anh explains that his family is from the north. In 1954, when he was eight, his father died. Since his mother had relatives living in central Vietnam, they moved south. He was drafted 16 years later, in 1970.

General Chi interjects that there were only three options open to young southern draftees: they could go into the army, they could go over to "the liberated zone," or they could evade the draft by going underground or resorting to a self-inflicted deferrable wound.

"I joined the army," says Mr. Anh, "because I needed the money to support my family."

Mr. Hiu explains that he is from Cu Chi, but had been sent to school in Saigon. "I was too young to understand the war," he says, "I got drafted, and I went."

"After the war, I thought about leaving," says Mr. Anh. "I had no use for communism. I was afraid of the communists — we'd been told there would be a bloodbath — but I couldn't figure a way to get my family out. I'm not sorry now that I stayed. Life these days is harder than before, but our spirit is better. We are rebuilding our country."

Mr. Hiu explains that not everyone has adjusted so well. Some former soldiers have quit the factory, and some have even left the country. In one case, he says, two workers tried to escape the country by boat, but were caught and arrested; later they were rehired by the factory and still work there.

What were the re-education camps like, we ask. Material life was poor, they respond, but the cadre were well behaved. "We could receive letters and even visits from relatives," says Mr. Anh. "It was better than marching." Was he forced to dig up old mines, I ask. He looks at me with a puzzled smile. "Of course not," he replies.

"We've been asking you questions all afternoon," says John. "Do you have any questions you want to ask us?"

"Do you think that what we are saying is just propaganda?" Mr. Anh asks. The bluntness of the question is disarming. I don't know what to say. Though the latitude we've been given to roam the streets on our own time has been unexpected, it has certainly occurred to me on numerous occasions that we are not likely to be formally introduced to people who are going to badmouth the way things are.

"Why do you ask?" I reply.

"Well," he says, "This is Sunday — my day off. I don't mind coming here and talking to you, but if you think what I am saying is just propaganda, then I'd rather be home with my wife and family."

After supper, John, Bruce and I go for a walk in a part of town we have not explored yet. It reminds me of Old Hanoi, though the streets are much wider. Once again, away from the downtown hotels, the cyclo drivers and beggars are nowhere to be seen. John buys a bunch of Buddhist prayer money from an old woman in a small shop. I notice Nestlé's candy bars for sale, along with German and Swiss chocolates.

Two middleaged couples are walking down the street just in front of us. I recognize them as part of a delegation of about 20 Russians staying at the Cuu Long. We have yet to get any of the Russians even to make eye contact with us, even when riding the tiny elevator up to the hotel restaurant. Out on the street, they are rude, pushy and loud. They remind me of Americans — except that the women look like potato dumplings. Even as I think it, I realize I am resorting to ethnic stereotyping, but by God, these two women *do* look like potato dumplings. And they *are* rude and obnoxious. And why in the hell won't any of them even say hello to us? That's just basic courtesy.

Officially, the Russians are the socialist comrades and allies of the Vietnamese. Every formal inquiry into Soviet-Vietnamese relations has yielded the same stock reply. But unofficially, we have gotten the sense that the Vietnamese may not be all that fond of the Russians. For one thing, we have learned that the Vietnamese have a special name for the Russians. It means "the Americans without money."

Later, I walk up to the square alone. The black Amerasian boy and the white Amerasian girl are both there, together with a full-blooded Vietnamese girl who speaks a little English. She tells me her name is Truong Ngoc Sanh, age 17. The black Amerasian is Nguyen Ngoc Tuan, age 15, and the white Amerasian is Nguyen Thi My Huong, age 14. Huong has stepped a few feet away from the others at my approach, as if she is distrustful or afraid of me. I can get her to smile if I wink or make a face, but her face clouds over quickly each time.

Sanh asks if I can get her some shampoo.

"Why shampoo?" I ask.

"To wash my hair," she replies.

"How about if I give you money to buy shampoo?"

"No good."

"Why not?"

"Can't buy good shampoo."

"Well, the only shampoo I have is the shampoo we bought today at the market," I reply.

"Market?" she says, pointing toward Nguyen Hue Boulevard.

"Yes."

She makes a sour face and shakes her head. "You give me pants," she says, tugging at my trouser leg.

"These pants?"

"Okay!" she says, smiling.

"They're too big for you," I reply.

"I fix," she says.

"How can I walk back to the hotel without any pants on?" I ask. She laughs at this, but is clearly disappointed.

So am I. This is the first time I've really been hustled by any of the children in the square.

"Why is Huong called 'My'?" I ask Sanh. "Does it mean 'American'?" Sanh nods her head yes. "Who gave her that name?" I ask.

The two girls confer in Vietnamese. "Her father," Sanh replies.

"Does she know who her father is?" I ask.

Another conference. "Mother have exit papers," Sanh says. "Huong go America in four months. Go to be with father."

"Where does her father live?" I ask. Sanh translates. Huong shrugs her shoulders, indicating that she doesn't know.

"What is her father's name?" I ask.

Huong takes my pad and pen. Laboriously, in large uneven block letters, she writes: ENTONISTONI.

"That his name?" I ask. She nods yes. "His whole name?" She nods yes again. Are there really exit papers, I wonder, is there a father waiting to receive her after 14 long years? Or is it just the pipedream of a lonely child with no future? Reason tells me to let it drop, but my heart can't quite let go. I've heard so many sad stories. Perhaps just once, I might be able to help.

"Tell Huong to ask her mother to give me her father's name and address," I tell Sanh, "Tell her to bring me the exit papers." *If* there are papers, perhaps they will indicate the father's name and address. *If* Huong's mother knows the father's name and address, *maybe* I can locate him when I get back to the states. Maybe, just maybe, there would be something I could do to help.

"You be here tomorrow?" Sanh asks.

"Not tomorrow," I reply. "Tomorrow I go Tay Ninh. Next day—I come here day after tomorrow. At night."

Above: Our first meeting with our host, General Tran Kinh Chi, in the offices of the Commission for Investigation into War Crimes. From left: John Balaban, Bruce Weigl, W.D. Ehrhart, Ngo Thi Troan (chief of the Commission's Foreign Relationship Section), General Kinh Chi, Mr. Quang (interpreter). (Photo courtesy of staff photographer, Commission of Investigation into War Crimes, Socialist Republic of Vietnam, hereafter referred to as CIWC.)

Right: General Tran Kinh Chi, now a civilian with a rank equivalent to vice minister, served as vice president of the war crimes commission. Knowing nothing of us, he was initially wary and formal, but as the trip progressed, he proved to be a genial and solicitous companion. (Photo CIWC.)

Top: Hotel rooms in Hanoi are primitive (light and telephone did not work) but cared for. *Above*: Hanoi's electric trolleys were put in by the French in the early 1900s; the newest cars are probably early 1940s. (Photos W.D. Ehrhart.)

Opposite, top: Visiting Ho Chi Minh's mausoleum. From left: Nguyen Hoang (bureau chief for the commission), John Balaban, Mrs. Troan, Bruce Weigl, W.D. Ehrhart, and Duong Van Loan, our interpreter. (Photo CIWC.) *Middle*: During our visit to the Palace of Children, these costumed kids put on a two-hour performance of singing and dancing. Afterwards, I recited a poem in English, which Miss Loan then said in Vietnamese. The man at center-right is the school's director. (Photo John Balaban.) *Bottom*: A high point of the trip was our audience with Te Hanh. From left: Te Hanh, Captain Vuong Trong of the Vietnamese Army, Miss Loan, Mrs. Troan, Bruce Weigl (facing away), and another member of the Vietnamese Writers' Union. (Photo W.D. Ehrhart.)

Top: We encountered several pagodas in religious use in Hanoi, but also saw several like this one in Old Hanoi that had long since been converted for housing and retail shops. *Above*: Private vendors of produce are everywhere to be seen in the narrow streets of Old Hanoi, a district that predates the arrival of the French by many centuries. (Photos W.D. Ehrhart.)

Top: Unlike the brash and aggressive cyclo drivers in Ho Chi Minh City who still remember the "boom times" during the war, the cyclo drivers of Hanoi are a laid-back bunch. *Above*: More numerous even than the street vendors are the bicyclists. Motor vehicles are few in Hanoi, but bicycles, affordable and efficient, are everywhere. (Photos W.D. Ehrhart.)

Top: Here, we meet with representatives from the SINCO Sewing Machine Factory in Ho Chi Minh City, all of them former junior officers in the old Saigon army. Clockwise, from the foreground: Le Kieu (director of the War Crimes Exhibit in Ho Chi Minh City), five factory staff, General Kinh Chi, W.D. Ehrhart, John Balaban, Doan Duc Luu (interpreter), and Bruce Weigl. (Photo CIWC.) *Above*: Ho Chi Minh City has many more motor vehicles than Hanoi—a legacy of the American presence. This little three-wheeled Lambretta can carry up to 13 people with rooftop cargo. (Photo W.D. Ehrhart.)

 Opposite, left: In November, 1963, fleeing from a U.S.-backed coup d'état, Ngo Dinh Diem and his brother Ngo Dinh Nhu tried to hide in this Catholic cathedral in Cholon, but were discovered and executed shortly thereafter. *Middle*: Flowering bushes like these along Nguyen Hue Boulevard, sprouting from rooftops and balconies, were everywhere in Ho Chi Minh City. *Right*: A residence for several hundred people under construction in Ho Chi Minh City's District Ten. (Photos W.D. Ehrhart.)

Top: Perhaps because of the high number of Catholics in the south, Christmas is still celebrated in Ho Chi Minh City. This tailor's shop was appropriately decorated for the season. When the tailor saw me with my camera, he insisted on getting into the picture. *Above*: Like well-preserved dinosaurs, these late 1950s and early 1960s American automobiles lined both sides of Nguyen Hue Boulevard for several blocks. I never saw any of them underway and never did learn why they were there or what they were used for. (Photos W.D. Ehrhart.)

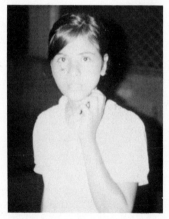

Top: Lunchtime at the Rehabilitation Center for Malnourished Orphans in Ho Chi Minh City. Most of these kids were terrified of the big strangers, but the boy in the clown hat wordlessly took my hand, joining our tour of the hospital. I never did find out where he got his party hat or why he was wearing it. *Above, left*: Truong Ngoc Sanh, 17 (left), and Nguyen Ngoc Tuan, 15, an Amerasian. Though Sanh commanded only a few words of English, she served as "interpreter" for Tuan and Huong (next photo) during our evenings together. *Above, right*: Nguyen Thi My Huong, 14, an Amerasian girl I met in a small plaza in downtown Ho Chi Minh City. Most Vietnamese have three names. Huong had a fourth name, *My*, Vietnamese for American. Literally, it means "beautiful." (Photos W.D. Ehrhart.)

Top: With the People's Fatherland Front, Ho Chi Minh City. From left: Pham Van Ba (Front vice president), W.D. Ehrhart, Doan Duc Luu, John Balaban, Bruce Weigl, General Kinh Chi, former Saigon general Nguyen Huu Hanh. (Photo CIWC.) *Above*: Selling sugar cane in Cholon. (Photo W.D. Ehrhart.)

Opposite, left: Harvard-educated economist Nguyen Xuan Oanh held several high-level posts in Saigon during the mid-1960s including, briefly, the office of premier. He is now an advisor to the People's Fatherland Front. (Photo John McAuliff.) *Right*: Former Viet Cong agent Thieu Thi Tao, 35, in front of a captured U.S. tank on the grounds of the War Crimes Exhibit in Ho Chi Minh City, spent six years in Saigon prisons. (Photo W.D. Ehrhart.)

Top: During our visit to Cu Chi, we crawled through a section of the tunnels still kept open. I didn't like the experience very much, and emerged from the hot, close darkness with enormous relief. Here, Tran Thi Bich, 28, is about to offer me a hand up. During the war, Miss Bich grew up in the tunnels, living in them from age 8 to 18. Now she is a rising member of the Communist Party in Cu Chi District. *Above*: W.D. Ehrhart inspecting a bomb crater half-filled with stagnant water. Large areas of Vietnam were devastated by B-52s engaged in what was called "carpet bombing." The bombs from three aircraft in close formation at high altitude could chew up a patch of land a mile long and half a mile wide. The Vietnamese have done a remarkable job of repairing the physical scars of the war, but many areas such as this one in Cu Chi District still look much as they did in 1975. (Photos Bruce Weigl.)

Top: The shallow hold of this boat on a small river in Cu Chi District is filled with threshed rice. We had come to see the remains of a ferry said to have been sunk by soldiers of the Saigon army in 1964, killing several hundred civilians. When we arrived at the river, the woman in the boat was filling baskets with rice, which she carried two at a time to a house 300 meters away, over and over again. She was still patiently and laboriously unloading rice when we left an hour later. *Above*: As we were inspecting B-52 bomb craters (see opposite) in Cu Chi, this pony cart came trotting down the road, collar bells jangling merrily. I don't recall ever having seen a horse in Vietnam during my 13 months there as a young Marine. (Photos W.D. Ehrhart.)

Above: Perhaps the most colorful and striking building in Vietnam: the Holy See of the Cao Dai religion, Tay Ninh City. A messianic sect founded in the 1920s, Cao Dai combines elements of several major religions. The political power of the Cao Dai was broken in the mid-1950s by Ngo Dinh Diem, but two-thirds of the population of Tay Ninh Province remain active believers.

Left: The three major saints of the Cao Dai are Sun Yatsen, Victor Hugo and Nguyen Binh Khiem, here depicted in this life-sized painting hanging in the vestibule of the cathedral in Tay Ninh City. (Photos W.D. Ehrhart.)

Top: The Pagoda of the Sleeping Buddha in Vung Tau perches on a hillside high above the South China Sea. This photo shows only a small part of the Buddha, which is made of highly polished solid stone and is easily thirty feet long. *Above*: Through these gates and around the bend in the road lies *Cam Pu Chia*, or Cambodia. The village of Tan Lap, Tay Ninh Province, where this border crossing is located, saw heavy fighting during the Pol Pot years, but the border provinces have been peaceful since Pol Pot was driven from power. (Photos W.D. Ehrhart.)

Top: Shrines honoring Ho Chi Minh, here flanked by portraits of Marx and Lenin, can be found in every state building. *Above*: Peasants threshing rice with a manually-powered machine in Tay Ninh Province. *Right*: Catholic church in Ho Chi Minh City, called the Pink Cathedral for its rose-colored bricks, at one end of what Americans knew as Tu Do Street. (Photos W.D. Ehrhart.)

Tay Ninh Province

Today we are going to Tay Ninh. Land of Black Widow Mountain and the once-vast Michelin rubber plantations. Home of the Cao Dai, that curious messianic religious sect whose three principal saints are Victor Hugo, Sun Yat-sen, and the 16th century philosopher-poet Nguyen Binh Khiem, who once wrote, "So many times I have known success and defeat that I have learned to despise honors and to choose a life of peace." I am looking forward to getting out into the countryside again. Except for Hue City during the Tet Offensive in the last month before I came home, my own experience during the war had little to do with cities.

We are supposed to leave at 5 a.m. — it will be a long drive, over 100 kilometers — but our hosts have trouble locating a car for us, and we do not get underway until nearly 7 a.m. General Chi and Luu ride with us. Mr. Kieu, Mr. Giai and Miss Phuong follow in a second car.

As we ride along, General Chi asks about the conditions of poor people in the United States. He has heard that one-third of Americans live in poverty. Yes, we explain, there *are* poor people in the United States — far too many for a country as wealthy as ours — but we don't think it is as many as one-third; perhaps one-fifth. Are blacks still treated as second-class citizens, he asks. Yes, we reply, often they are, but racial discrimination is not so bad now as when we were children; we hope things will continue to improve.

In Vietnam, the general says, all people are treated equally. Everyone has the same opportunities and the same benefits. "Some SINCO workers make more than I do," he adds, as if to prove his point.

We have heard this argument several times since we've been in Vietnam. We have also heard younger Vietnamese dispute this claim. Privately, a low echelon government employee has told us that people like the general — those with the rank of vice minister or its equivalent and above — receive certain benefits like the use of a car, housing, and better medical care that reflect a new form of classism. "Given how poor we are," this person has said, "we cannot afford to have such a privileged class."

Certainly, the general did have the use of a private car in Hanoi, which he placed at our disposal. Just as certainly, he has had more than a little difficulty arranging transportation for us here in the south. Beyond that, I can speculate not at all about just how privileged the general may or may not be. What would he make of poor people with television sets, I wonder.

John asks if the Vietnamese would ever allow Soviet combat troops to be stationed in Vietnam. Of course not, the general replies, suggesting that the Vietnamese did not spend a century fighting the French and the Americans only to hand their country over to the Russians. What about Danang and Cam Ranh Bay, we ask — former United States bases now used by Soviet air and naval forces. "That is not the same," the general replies, though he doesn't elaborate.

Instead, he points to the looming mass of Nui Ba Den — Black Widow Mountain — its peak visible above a heavy ground haze. Impossible to miss, it juts up 986 meters above the flat surrounding plain. The Americans had a helicopter base on top of the mountain, the general explains, but were never aware that the Viet Cong had bases all around the foot of the mountain and even in caves and tunnels inside of it. At various times, he says, the VC had as many as three divisions living underground right under the noses of the Americans.

Finally, after a two-hour drive, we arrive at the provincial People's Committee headquarters in Tay Ninh City, where we are met by the committee's vice president — the equivalent of a lieutenant governor — the committee's information officer, and several other men. After the introductions are made, and the coffee and tea served, the information officer pulls out a thick stack of yellow legal sheets. It is a *very* thick stack of typed notes, and I realize with a sinking feeling that we are in for a very long morning.

We are told that Tay Ninh Province has a population of 750,000, and that the province shares a 240 kilometer border with Kampuchea. The information officer recites a long list of American "war crimes" in Tay Ninh, including B-52 raids, napalm, chemical warfare, destruction of pagodas, two-thirds of all forests destroyed, 21,000 people killed between 1964 and 1975 . . .

After 15 minutes of this, my head is swimming in statistics. It reminds me of our first few days in Hanoi, before General Chi realized he was doing more harm than good by lecturing at us. And it is all made more unbearable by the plodding, pedantic pace of the provincial information officer's delivery.

Soon, however, an unintended diversion is offered in the form of an assistant who begins to try to put up a wall map to illustrate the areas of the province denuded by chemical defoliation. Without tape or thumbtacks, he is having the devil of a time, turning the map this way and that, trying to stick the map to the wall by sheer force of will alone. Still, he betrays no sense of impatience or frustration, and at last he manages to wedge the top edge of the map beneath a framed picture already hanging on the wall.

Time and again, I have witnessed small episodes like this one, each reinforcing the fact that the Vietnamese have not even the simplest of the day-to-day goods and amenities we take for granted. Time and again, I have watched them persist until they find a solution. Having hung the map, the man turns to a slide projector to show pictures of babies suffering deformities resulting from the use of chemical defoliants. The projector has an automatic feed button on it, but it breaks immediately, so he patiently feeds each slide into the projector manually, one slide at a time.

Meanwhile, the information officer tells us that the province has exercised "a policy of generosity" toward the 30,000 collaborators from Tay Ninh. Most "puppets," he tells us, received no more than three months in the re-education camps. Two doctors who were once in the Saigon army are now members of the People's Committee, he says.

What about the Cao Dai religion, we ask, has it been suppressed? No, he replies, the present policy is to "respect the superstitions of the people," and two-thirds of the population of the province still actively practice Cao Dai. It is only when reactionaries take advantage of the people's superstition to resist the revolution that the government must intervene. Since 1975, he says, ten reactionary plots have been uncovered in Tay Ninh.

Then he tells us that Tay Ninh is the most exposed province of Vietnam because it is bordered on three sides by Kampuchea. During the Pol Pot years, Tay Ninh Province bore the brunt of Pol Pot's attacks, in addition to having to care for the 30,000 Cambodian refugees who fled to Tay Ninh to escape Pol Pot's depredations. He explains that later we will drive up to the village of Tan Lap near the Kampuchean border. Here, he says, on the night of September 24–25, 1977, Pol Pot's forces killed 1,492 Vietnamese civilians.

"For years, we suffered raids like this," the province vice president interjects. "If you are living in your house peacefully and you are attacked, you have to defend yourself. That is true all over the world."

At last the information officer seems to exhaust his notes, and we pile into the cars for the 45-kilometer drive up to Tan Lap. We have three cars now, our two plus one carrying the province officials. I find myself thinking of my friend Larry Heinemann, author of *Close Quarters*, a novel set in Tay Ninh. How many times had Larry driven this same road in his armored personnel carrier? The red dust blanketing the road is six inches thick and powdery fine, and our cars kick up vast clouds of the stuff.

I had forgotten the dust of Vietnam: seeping into your nostrils and under your fingernails, coating your clothes and clogging every pore in your body. There was a time when I thought I would never be able to wash the dust of Vietnam from my skin. As we ride along the narrow, bumpy, dirt road, I think of the ancient Vietnamese folk poem: "A clear mind spreads like the wind; by the Lo waterfalls, free and high, you wash away the dust of life."

But a flat tire on one of the other cars brings a screeching halt to my reveries. We pull off to the side of the road. There is not a single spare tire among our three cars, but fortunately we are in the midst of a small hamlet and patching equipment is available.

While we wait, I notice a group of about 30 or 40 young children doing organized calisthenics in a nearby schoolyard. They notice us, too, and soon we are surrounded by a throng of curious kids clearly amazed by the white-skinned intruders. I want to get a photograph of the kids, but the instant they see my camera, they all line up as if for a formal class portrait and the spontaneity of the moment is lost. I wander off and soon discover an old man tending a flock of white ducks grazing on the stubble of a partially flooded rice field that has already been harvested.

The tire fixed, we are on our way again. Suddenly, the road becomes level macadam and broadens out to about five times its previous width. We stop and get out. All of this was once the largest U.S. Special Forces base in the province, General Chi explains, sweeping his arm in a broad flat arc across a landscape devoid of anything but a few scrubby trees and bushes. Before that, it had been a forest, but when the base was built, he says, the trees were killed with chemicals and the whole area bulldozed flat. "This is all that remains," he adds, tapping the blacktop surface with his foot, "This used to be the airstrip for the base."

We get back into the cars, and then we reach the end of the runway and are back on the narrow dirt road with the red dust billowing around us like a biblical pillar of smoke.

At Tan Lap village, only a few kilometers from the Kampuchean border, we get out of the cars and walk to a hamlet several hundred meters from the road. This is where Pol Pot attacked on that night in September 1977, the provincial vice president tells us. As we talk, a small crowd of villagers gathers around us. One of the women points down the trail toward another woman on a bicycle; she calls out, and the woman on the bicycle changes course and comes over to us.

"Yes, I was here that night," the woman on the bicycle tells us. "They crept in without making a sound. They used axes and clubs and knives. No guns. They didn't want our militia to hear them. I was awakened by the screams of my neighbors. My brother and uncle were killed, butchered like pigs. I ran away and hid."

Did the villagers do anything to provoke the attack? "We never did a thing," she replies emphatically. "We never did them any harm. They just attacked us. Pol Pot."

Later, we drive to the border itself. There is a small Vietnamese army garrison, and a wooden checkpoint with several uniformed guards, but there is not much else to see. The road passes through the checkpoint, then makes a long slow curve to the left and disappears around a clump of scrawny trees. The actual border, the general tells us, is another kilometer or two down the road. So much for my notion of stepping across the border, just to say I've been to Kampuchea.

On the way back to Tay Ninh City, the unlucky car of the provincial officials sustains a second flat tire. This time, we are in the middle of nowhere. The four officials redistribute themselves among the other two cars and the driver is left to fend for himself.

In our little sedan, we now have seven people. It is *very* hot and very dusty, and the exhaust fumes coming up through the floorboards are almost overwhelming. I cannot remember ever having suffered a more uncomfortable ride, yet our hosts make no apologies. I am finding myself perpetually amazed at the grace and stoicism with which the Vietnamese accept these constant setbacks: flat tires, clogged fuel pumps, broken slide projectors, maps with no tape or tacks. Such things, it seems, are simply the facts of life in a poor country, and there is no use getting upset about them.

And there is yet another flat tire. It is on the other car. We stop while our hosts confer, then we go on, leaving the second car and all of its occupants stranded by the side of the road. By the time we get back to the

People's Committee headquarters, I can think of nothing but getting out of Tay Ninh Province.

Waiting for us, however, are several large basins of cold water. The general ladles water over my head as I bend down above one of the basins. The water revives my flagging spirits somewhat, and a cold beer further revitalizes me.

But lunch is eaten in near-total silence. The atmosphere is more strained than at any previous time during the trip. Aside from our chance encounter with the woman in Tan Lap village, we have driven a long way from Ho Chi Minh City, and eaten a great deal of dust, for very little of substance. The silence of the others suggests that I am not the only one who feels this way. As we eat, those we have left strewn along the road to the Kampuchean border come straggling in, looking horse-whipped and dog-tired.

The general suggests that we all take a nap, but I want to go down to the nearby river to take some photographs. I ask the information officer, and he says it's okay. I walk out to the main gate of the compound, and as I approach I smile at the young policeman standing guard. He smiles back, but steps into my path. I hold up my camera, point toward the river only 100 meters away, and explain that I'm just going to take a few pictures, I'll be right back, I've got permission. He doesn't understand any English, and as I step forward again, he firmly places his hand on my arm while his other hand goes down to the barrel of the AK-47 he is carrying on his shoulder combat-style.

For a moment, my temper almost breaks loose. Hey, dude, I'm a free man, I think angrily, who the hell do you think you are? Then I realize the absurdity of what I am thinking. This isn't my country, and I don't make the rules. Besides, he's got a loaded AK, and I'm armed only with an Olympus XA-2. I shake my head, then turn back, intent upon finding Luu to come and straighten this fellow out.

Instead, I come upon the general first. He is lying on a double-bed in a second-floor room. He glances up as I look in and gestures to me sharply, patting the bed beside him. The general doesn't speak any English, so I can't explain to him what has happened, and he continues to slap the bed with the flat of his hand. Obviously, he wants me to lie down and take a nap. So much for taking pictures of the river, I think, giving up and lying down beside the general. He whacks me on the ankles, indicating that I'm supposed to take off my shoes, then he rolls over and goes to sleep.

I fall asleep, too, and am awakened about a half-hour later by Luu.

I explain to Luu what happened with the policeman. Luu laughs apologetically, perhaps a little embarrassed. "He was just doing his job." he says, "He didn't understand who you are."

Downstairs again, the provincial information officer—armed with more yellow sheets of paper—launches into a long explanation of the progress Tay Ninh Province has made since the end of the war. Even the general seems to be having trouble staying awake. "This guy could put a speed-freak to sleep," I write in my notepad. Meanwhile, Luu's translation goes roughly like this: "Well, now he's telling you what he already told you this morning. Don't bother to write any of this down; you've heard all of this before. This, too. Oh, fuck, I don't believe this." It is impossible to keep a straight face. I keep having to cover my mouth with my hand, to look up at the ceiling or down at the table. I don't dare look at John or Bruce, knowing they must also be right on the edge of breaking down with laughter. The information officer rattles on laboriously for nearly an hour, his voice plodding and monotonous, Luu's barely contained frustration increasingly evident in the running commentary of his "translation."

Finally, the information officer informs us that we will now pile back into the cars and drive another 45 kilometers—one way—to inspect a new reservoir and hydroelectric dam in the northeast corner of the province. I practically holler, "No!" But Luu is way ahead of me. Without consulting us or the general, he replies immediately in Vietnamese, and the general joins the conversation, too. I can't understand what is being said, but it seems clear that Luu and the general are no more inclined to take another long, hot, dusty ride than I am.

Whatever is being said, it works. Instead, the officials of Tay Ninh decide to take us to the province exhibition hall—where we see a scale model of the new reservoir, a stuffed cow, a stuffed pig, a stuffed chicken, and an enormous and graphically gruesome mural depicting the suffering of the Kampucheans under Pol Pot—then to a new hospital on the outskirts of the city. Then we come back to the committee's headquarters where John, Bruce and I are each presented with a small carved wooden statue of the Laughing Buddha.

Each buddha is boxed and gift-wrapped, and as we open our presents, the province vice president explains that the Laughing Buddha is the symbol of prosperity and happiness. He hopes, he says, that these buddhas will bring both to each of us. He speaks awkwardly and with apparent feeling, and it occurs to me that the officials of Tay Ninh have had no more idea of what to do with us and for us today than had General

Chi and his staff when we'd first arrived in Hanoi. I thank him as graciously as I can, hoping that my day-long impatience and boredom haven't been too evident.

As we drive out the gate, I notice that the same policeman is still on duty. "You want me to scold him for you?" Luu asks, nudging me.

"No," I reply, "Ask the general if we can visit the Holy See of the Cao Dai." The general readily agrees.

The Cao Dai religion was founded in 1926 by a Vietnamese visionary who believed that all religions are one. At the time, the Vietnamese were suffering a terrible economic depression, made worse by French exploitation, and people were literally starving to death by the thousands. Struggling to survive, finding neither solace nor answers in the old ways, the people of Tay Ninh Province readily flocked to the new religion, which incorporates elements of every major religion in the world. By the time of the French Indochina War, the sect had become a political power with its own army, but the temporal power of the Cao Dai was finally broken in the mid-1950s by Ngo Dinh Diem.

The "Vatican" of the Cao Dai, called the Holy See, is a spacious compound of numerous buildings and wide parade grounds enclosed by high walls. The largest of the buildings is the main cathedral, a truly fabulous structure that looks like a cross between a Catholic cathedral and a Chinese pagoda. The dominant color is white, with red tile roofing, but blues, reds, yellows and greens leap at the eye from every angle. External arches are bordered by brightly colored designs of fruit and flowers, snakes and dragons entwine many of the pillars, and each window is ornately decorated with twisting vines and flowers. In the center of each window, enclosed in a triangle, is the single all-seeing eye of the universe. Various life-sized statues of people flank the main entrance, and above it, enclosed in a blue square, is another representation of the all-knowing eye, white lines of light radiating away from it. The multiplicity of designs, colors and symbols is staggering. The flag of the Socialist Republic of Vietnam flies just above the main entrance but below the all-knowing eye.

Inside, in the vestibule, is a large painting depicting the three saints: Hugo, Sun Yat-sen, and the poet Khiem. They appear to be floating on clouds. Suspended in front of them is a tablet with characters that I take to be Chinese — or perhaps a mixture of Chinese and Nom, the old Vietnamese character language. Interspersed among these characters, Hugo is just finishing writing the words: "Dieu et Humanité, Amour et Justice."

We are met by an old woman in a white robe who is one of the priests. The general bows respectfully and we all follow his lead. Taking off our shoes, we enter the main sanctuary. It reminds me of the inside of a European cathedral — the whole interior leading up to the altar is open, with no benches or pews — but the floor is polished to a glistening sheen and colorful draperies hang along the walls. The altar itself is a fantastic array of decorated tables, pillars wreathed by serpents, brass urns and painted statues. And above it all, at the highest point of the altar, dominating the inner sanctuary, is a huge blue globe with the all-knowing eye right in the center of it, staring out at the faithful.

It is as though we've leaped into another world — unearthly, surreal, the stuff of fairy tales — but this is a living, active religion with at least a half a million adherents. As we put on our shoes again and get ready to leave, I notice that the general bows once again to the priest, then places a contribution of money into a box by the door.

Halfway back to Ho Chi Minh City, we stop in a small hamlet straddling the road. The general is thirsty and has spotted a roadside vendor — an old woman selling fresh sugarcane juice. He offers to spot us all a round of drinks. The woman's stand is right along the road, she and her stand are covered in dust, nothing looks too sanitary, I can't imagine her boiling the water from which the ice is made, and I keep remembering McAuliff's admonition not to drink anything that isn't bottled or boiled.

But once again, I am embarrassed to express my reservations, I am absolutely out of my mind with thirst, and everyone else seems prepared to risk it. What the hell, I think, I seem to have survived the orangeade in Cu Chi the other day. The woman squeezes glass after glass of juice, stuffing the raw sugarcane stalks into an ancient press. We all take turns helping her turn the press's crank while she and the general have a conversation about I don't know what, but it makes her laugh uproariously. The drinks are delicious, sweet and cold.

Even with the break, however, by the time we get back to Ho Chi Minh City and the hotel, I am covered with dust inside and out, my eyes sting as though I've had my head stuck up somebody's muffler for about three days, and I am utterly exhausted. The hotel restaurant is closed, but I don't care. I head immediately for my room and the bathtub.

An hour later, as I am drying off, the telephone rings. It is Linda Trigg, an Australian woman I had met several days earlier in the hotel bar. We hadn't had time to talk then, but I'd suggested that we get together later. I am pleased to hear her voice. She wants me to come up to her room for a drink. "I've got some very cold Foster's Lager up here," she says.

"I'll be right up," I reply.

Linda and three other Australians are staying at the Cuu Long. One is a member of the Australian embassy staff in Bangkok. Linda and the other two work for the Australian High Commissioner for Refugees. They are in Ho Chi Minh City for three weeks interviewing Vietnamese requesting resettlement to Australia. At this late date, she has already explained, only people who already have relatives living in Australia can be considered for emigration. Six days a week, she and her colleagues, each with an interpreter assigned by the Vietnamese government, interview applicants. Interviews are often awkward, she has said, because of the government interpreters. Applicants often seem afraid to speak openly, perhaps fearing reprisals from the government, and she is not always convinced that the interpreters are rendering accurate translations of what is being said by either party. "Some interpreters seem to be more sensitive and understanding than others," she has told me, "but you never know which interpreter you'll get until you show up in the morning."

There are two round-trip flights into Ho Chi Minh City each week from Bangkok, one on Monday and one on Thursday. Unlike the Australians, who come and stay for a period of weeks each time, working long hours to interview as many people as possible, she has told me that the American immigration officials working with the Orderly Departure Program fly in on the morning flight, conduct their interviews at the airport itself, and fly out when the plane returns to Bangkok in the afternoon. For all of the hoopla the Reagan administration has made about the Vietnamese not cooperating with ODP, it strikes me as a remarkably leisurely pace at which to work.

"Where did you get this stuff?" I ask Linda as I empty one Foster's and open another.

"We bring it with us," she replies, laughing. "Diplomatic mail. Nobody makes beer like we do — not even the Germans. Certainly not the Vietnamese." She asks me about the trip to Tay Ninh, and I tell her about the Holy See of the Cao Dai and about the woman we spoke to in the village of Tan Lap.

"I don't see any way our encounter with that woman could have been staged," I remark. "I think she was telling the truth."

"She probably was," Linda replies. She explains that there are about 8,000 Cambodians living in Australia. "They hide in their houses and peek out now and then," she says, "They're all terrified, even now, even in Australia. They're just waiting for someone to come and take them away. We can't communicate with them. We can't get them to integrate at all. There's no community to organize around, no one to act as a spokesperson for them. Pol Pot killed anyone with any sort of skill or training or education."

She explains that she has just finished several months of interviewing Cambodian refugees in the camps along the Thai border. "I hadn't expected to hear what I heard," she says. "I didn't hear a single story about ill treatment or undisciplined behavior among the Vietnamese troops. People told me instance after instance of Vietnamese soldiers sharing their food with them, providing medical care from their own first aid kits. It's really quite remarkable."

"Then why do the Kampucheans want to leave?" I ask.

"They're afraid of Pol Pot," she replies. "They're afraid that the moment the Vietnamese leave, Pol Pot will come back."

"Is that likely?" I ask.

"Well, let me put it this way," she says, "you should see the Khmer Rouge 'refugee' camps. They're not refugee camps at all. They're armed guerrilla bases. Listen, I'm just talking as a private individual here, this is just my own feelings based on what I've seen, but this so-called 'democratic front' your President Reagan keeps harping about is nothing but a farce. Pol Pot's guerrillas are the only viable military force in town. And if and when the Vietnamese leave, they'll be back all right. They'll be back with a vengeance."

New Year's Eve

The Vice President of the People's Committee of Ho Chi Minh City greets us in a large reception room of the city's version of City Hall. He is the equivalent of a deputy mayor. As we eat tangerines and drink coffee, he explains that the committee governs the 12 districts of the city itself plus the surrounding six suburban districts. He talks about the problems the city has faced since the end of the war.

"Before liberation, almost all industrial necessities were imported. Now we suffer from shortages of raw materials, fuel and energy, and spare parts," he says, noting that many factory managers and other skilled people fled Vietnam in the last days of the war, "but we are working to overcome these problems. We can develop our own raw materials, but for this we need energy."

He explains that a 400,000-kilowatt hydroelectric plant is currently under construction; the first turbine will go on line in 1987, and the entire plant is scheduled for completion by 1990. An oil-fired 400,000-kilowatt powerplant is being built at Vung Tau, which will be fueled by offshore oil deposits now being developed with the help of the Soviets. Other smaller power projects in the 100,000-kilowatt range are also underway. Currently, he says, 60 to 70 percent of electricity and oil must be reserved for production, but the goal is to develop enough power for both industry and home use by the year 2000.

"We are also developing our own capacity to make spare parts," he says, explaining that importation of fertilizer and chemicals has to take precedence over cars and other vehicles. "We can't afford to buy new vehicles, but many vehicles left over from wartime are still running because we can make our own spare parts."

Food production is another problem. During the war, he explains, the six suburban districts surrounding the city were all "white zones" — what we would call free fire zones — which were totally devastated. Cu

162

Chi District was one of them. "Our goal," he says, "is to convert the 'white zones' into a 'green belt' capable of feeding the city." Currently, the yield is a little over one and a half crops a year, he says, but with the addition of the new reservoir in Tay Ninh Province—the one we *didn't* see yesterday—scheduled for completion in 1986, the yield should rise to two full crops per year. The long-range goal, he says, is to have three crops each year, but for this the Vietnamese need still more irrigation, tractors and fertilizer.

Social problems such as drugs and prostitution still remain from the war years, he continues, though the incidence has been greatly reduced and is "far less than in most western countries." Many of the one million unemployed in Saigon by the end of the war have been absorbed by state farms and factories, he says, but that problem too is not entirely solved. Yet another problem is the high birth rate. "We need better family planning," he says. "What you call women's liberation, I believe—that is really the same thing as family planning. Our slogan is, 'Two children is enough: delay marriage; if you are already married, delay childbirth.'"

He goes on to explain that there have been "many difficulties" in transferring from a private economy to a collective economy, most of which he attributes to "the long years of false propaganda and preconditioning in the south. Such a difficult transformation can't be done by force," he says, "but we had to learn that. After liberation, we tried to collectivize too rapidly. In some areas, the process went badly. Now we are trying to slow the process down, to collectivize through education rather than coercion. In the long run, the private sector cannot compete with the collectives in such things as irrigation, heavy equipment and pest control. We hope that people will see the benefits of collectivization and voluntarily offer their land to the collective." Currently, he says, 85 percent of the peasants and 80 percent of the land have already been collectivized.

In the industrial sector, he continues, the government immediately nationalized all major interests that had been abandoned by the "bourgeoisie" at the end of the war, but small industry is still operating on a mixed basis. "Skilled individual handicrafts like shoe repair should *not* be collectivized," he says. "We can achieve better production on an individual basis. Since 1980, handicrafts and light industry have increased their output by 20 percent. Socialism should lead to a higher standard of living; if it doesn't, then even *I* don't want socialism. We must be creative. The socialist economic policies of countries like the

Soviet Union and Czechoslovakia can't be applied to Vietnam without question. We must adapt to Vietnamese conditions."

Before we leave, he asks if we have any additional questions. What was his part in the war, we ask. He explains that he became a member of the Central Committee of the National Liberation Front in 1960, the year the NLF was founded, and that later he served as vice minister of foreign affairs in the provisional revolutionary government, established in 1969.

"Are Amerasian children discriminated against?" I ask.

"No," he replies, "there is no discrimination. Amerasian children are treated just like all other Vietnamese children. If the mother is living, the child is her responsibility. Orphans are cared for by the Ministry of War Invalids and Social Welfare."

But these children are half-American, I argue; they were fathered by the soldiers of the "imperialist aggressors" and their mothers were prostitutes or at least "collaborators." How is it possible that these children would *not* be discriminated against by other Vietnamese, even with the best efforts of the government?

"Yes," he replies. "Sometimes some people do discriminate against them. But this is only a small minority, and we are doing our best to overcome it. As you have learned in your own civil rights movement, it is difficult to legislate morality. We do care for these children. Most of them, I believe, have been successfully integrated into society."

During our lunch break, I am approached by a young cyclo driver I've seen before in the company of the Amerasian cyclo driver named "Jimmy." He tells me that Jimmy has been arrested for talking to us. When was he arrested, I ask. "Yesterday," the boy replies. "No have cyclo license."

"You need a license to drive a cyclo?"

"Yes."

"Well, was he arrested for talking with us, or was he arrested for driving a cyclo without a license?"

The boy looks puzzled, as if the distinction had not occurred to him until this moment. "You give me money?" he asks.

"What for? What about Jimmy?"

"My father very sick," he says. "Need medicine." He tells me that two of his brothers now live in Japan, and that he himself has an ODP number, but can't get an exit visa. His father, he says, was a pilot in the old Saigon air force, that he was recently arrested by the police and beaten up. "He very sick," he says. "I no have money for medicine."

Is this kid telling the truth, or is he just another street hustler like all the other street hustlers all over the world who tailor their pitches to suit their market? If Jimmy got arrested for talking to Americans, why is this kid willing to accost me openly on a busy street in broad daylight? Is it a mark of desperation, or have I simply been pegged as an easy touch? "You'd better move on," I reply, "or maybe they will arrest you, too."

In the afternoon, we hold a final critique and summary of the trip with General Chi, Mr. Kieu, Mr. Giai and Miss Phuong. "The door to Vietnam is open," says General Chi. "Normalization is not at hand, but we are ready whenever the United States is. In the meantime, exchanges of friends like this are good for building understanding. We want that very much."

He apologizes again for the misunderstanding over the rented black Chevrolet, explaining that they had simply assumed we could afford to pay for it. "You are college professors, teachers, published writers," he says. "We thought that must mean big salaries. We didn't understand until we got to know you. How can we sympathize if we do not understand? That is why visits like yours are important."

Then, as we drink iced Coca-Cola and eat cake — the first Western-style cake I've encountered here — the general presents us with two over-sized picturebooks, one with photos from the war, the other with scenic photos from peacetime Vietnam. They are high-quality books by Vietnamese standards, durable paper and binding materials being extremely scarce, and thus it is no small gesture. Each is inscribed to "Bruce, Balaban & E'hat," and signed "Kinh Chi."

Mr. Kieu then presents us each with a small lacquerware ashtray. "It isn't much," he says apologetically, "but we hope you will think of us each time you use it."

"Perhaps, someday, I will be able to come and visit you in the United States," adds General Chi.

Mr. Giai, nods his head in agreement, his face lit with a wide smile, his eyes brimming with tears. "Now we are friends," he says. "We will always be friends." He reaches out and touches my knee, giving my head a paternal shake with his other hand.

"Now we have a special treat for you," the general says. "The Fatherland Front has invited you to dinner tonight. I hope you haven't made any plans."

Waiting for us at a place called Friendship House are Mr. Ba of the Fatherland Front, General Hanh, a man named Nguyen Xuan Oanh, and several other men. The meal is another sumptuous feast of many courses, but the most amazing thing of all is the coconut cuckoo soup. Stripped of its husk but still in its shell, the whole coconut becomes the bowl. A three-inch circle has been cut in the top like a lid, and inside, cooked in a broth of coconut milk and vegetables, is a cuckoo bird. The feathers have been removed, but otherwise the bird is whole, including the head and feet. My initial revulsion at discovering a whole bird in my soup, and a cuckoo at that — I didn't even know people ate cuckoos — is forgotten with the first mouthful. As I eat the broth, I scrape the coconut meat — cooked by the hot broth — from the inside of the shell. The bird I dismember by hand and eat like a small chicken. The whole concoction is incredibly good.

I am seated next to General Hanh and across from Mr. Oanh. Mr. Oanh's English is impeccable, and he strikes me as an urbane and cultured man with a quick wit and a dry sense of humor. Where did he learn to speak English, I ask. At Harvard, he replies, explaining that he holds a Ph.D. in economics from Harvard and lived in the United States for ten years in the 1950s and early 1960s.

"Henry Kissinger was at Harvard then, wasn't he?" I ask.

"Yes," Mr. Oanh replies, rolling his eyes. "He and I were faculty colleagues."

"What did you think of him?" I ask.

"A vain and arrogant man," he replies. "He got carried away with himself, I think."

Mr. Oanh explains that he returned to Vietnam in 1963, after the overthrow of Diem, at the request of the new Saigon government. For the next several years, he held a succession of high-level government jobs, mostly having to do with the economy, and the monetary and banking systems. On two brief occasions, however, he served as premier of the old Republic of Vietnam. "Yes," he says, "for a short time, I was officially the premier — the equivalent of your president. But in reality, the generals still held all the power. There was really nothing I could do."

When Nguyen Van Thieu became president in 1967, he explains, he left the government altogether. "A detestable man," Mr. Oanh says of Thieu. "You know, in 1965, when I was premier, I proposed a plan to Secretary of Defense Robert McNamara for an American withdrawal from the war. I told him that prolonging the war would only work against United States interests." He stops and chuckles, almost as if enjoying a private joke. "McNamara dismissed me out of hand," he continues. "He simply couldn't conceive of an American defeat in Vietnam."

"They wouldn't ever listen to us," General Hanh interjects. "They had all the answers." His English isn't so good as Mr. Oanh's, and he often has to pause, searching for a word. Once, he explains, when he was deputy commander of II Corps, the famous American advisor John Paul Vann ordered him to replace one of his most senior aides with a man of Vann's choosing. General Hanh thought Vann was wrong, and told him so. "He threatened to cut off U.S. aid," says General Hanh, "and I was forced to make the change."

Another time, a different American advisor ordered General Hanh to call for B-52 raids on a certain area. The general flew over the area, and though he knew there were VC present, he determined that there were too many civilians to use B-52s. "I refused to call in B-52s," he says. He was subsequently relieved of his command, B-52s were called in by his replacement, and soon afterwards the entire area—including the local Saigon army garrison—went over to the Viet Cong side.

General Hanh has already explained why he stayed in Vietnam after the war, but I ask Mr. Oanh why *he* stayed.

"Well," he replies with a wry smile, "on his last trip to Saigon, Mr. Kissinger promised to get me out, but he never came back for me." At this, he laughs softly, then shrugs. "This is my country," he says, gesturing toward the other end of the table where General Chi, Mr. Ba and Mr. Kieu are seated, "These people need all the help they can get. They really don't know what they're doing sometimes." He mentions the current conversion from old dong to new dong. "And you still can't get change," he laughs. "I could have told them that wouldn't solve the problem, but nobody bothered to ask me. Now they're asking me to unscramble their mess for them."

"How did you end up working for the Fatherland Front?" I ask.

Immediately after the war, he explains, he was kept in detention—a sort of house arrest—for a year or so, but was eventually released and pretty much left alone. "My wife is a famous movie star," he says, "and some of my relatives fought in the resistance. I guess that didn't hurt." In 1982, thanks to a sympathetic editor at a quasi-independent newspaper, he published an article critical of the new regime's economic policies in the south. At first, both he and the editor got into trouble for it. "Oh, they accused us of treason," he laughs; "they wanted to throw us both in jail." But then some powerful people higher up read the article. "They decided I was making a lot of sense," he says, "so they offered me a job."

Later, as we are leaving, General Hanh asks me if I think President

Reagan will go ahead with the Strategic Defense Initiative, the so-called
Star Wars defense. I tell him that many American scientists have spoken
out against it, but that Reagan will probably get his way eventually.
General Hanh shakes his head slowly. "Nuclear war," he says, "Weapons
in space. It's insane. I'm afraid for my grandchildren."

"So am I," I reply.

"This war—Vietnam—this was nothing," he says. "If things continue, it will be the end. The end of everything."

Later, after we return to the hotel, I walk up to the square to try to
find Huong, Tuan and Sanh. I had told them two nights ago I would
meet them tonight. All three of them are there. "Does she have her
papers?" I ask Sanh, nodding toward Huong.

Huong smiles shyly and hands me a piece of brown paper with blue
graph lines on it. The sheet is folded into a tight triangle. It doesn't look
very official. I open it. One side of the sheet is filled with handwritten
words and figures that appear to be a makeshift conversion table, old
dong to new dong. The list continues onto the top of the reverse side.
Below the end of the list, handwritten in English, is the following
letter:

Ho Chi Minh City   November 19

1985

Dear Mr. Lee

I would like to request you about this thing—

I have received the document concerning my interest about mother
of a child whose father was an american citizen I already fill out the
enclosed questionnaire but I could not send to you until now because I
am so poor and haven't enouft money to send it

Could you help me if it is possible. I send you all document I have
and I hope to receive sooner your answer

Sincerely—

Nguyen Thi Wong

"This is all she has?" I ask Sanh.

She confers with Huong, then replies, "Yes."

"Jesus."

"What wrong?" Sanh asks.

"Nothing," I reply.

"Why you cry?" Sanh asks. Huong strokes my hair with her hand, as
if petting an animal she half-expects might turn on her at any moment.

It is all I can do to keep from coming unglued right in the middle of the square.

"I've got to go now," I blurt out quickly, "Come back tomorrow night. I see you tomorrow, okay?"

Back at the hotel, I place a call to Anne. The whopping bill I received for the call I made my first day in Ho Chi Minh City has kept me away from the telephone for a week. But tonight, I am feeling lonely and depressed and helpless, and I need to hear Anne's voice. It is New Year's morning back home. Anne tells me about the party she went to the night before — the annual New Year's Eve Loganstein Gala, the first one I've missed since before we were married. I don't tell her about Huong. "I'll be home in a few days," I say, "I love you."

I hang up and take Huong's scrap of paper up to Linda's room, knowing it is pointless. Linda reads the note, then hands it back. "It's worthless," she says. "There's not a thing I can do with it. There's not a thing *you* can do with it. Heartbreaking, isn't it? I deal with people like this all the time. Even if they manage to get on the ODP list, it only means they've been granted the right to an interview by your government or our government or whatever list they're on. It doesn't mean they're approved. But they don't understand that. They come for their interview, and they think they're home free. Sometimes it gets to me. This kid really got to you, didn't she? Well, look, mate, I've got something for you. I've been saving it for a special occasion."

She goes over to the refrigerator and pulls out a bottle of Australian champagne. "Happy New Year," she says, popping the cork.

Vung Tau

In my dream of the hydroplane
I'm sailing to Bien Hoa
the shrapnel in my thighs
like tiny glaciers.
I remember a flower,
a kite, a mannikin playing the guitar,
a yellow fish eating a bird, a truck
floating in urine, a rat carrying a banjo,
a fool counting the cards, a monkey praying,
a procession of whales, and far off
two children eating rice,
speaking French —
I'm sure of the children,
their damp flutes,
the long line of their vowels.

"Why French?" I ask Bruce.

"What?" he replies, startled.

"In your poem, 'Sailing to Bien Hoa,' why are the children speaking French?"

"I met some children near Hue one time," he says, "They were speaking French. I don't know why. Lots of Vietnamese still spoke French back then. What made you think of that?"

"The fork in the road back there — the sign on the left fork said 'Bien Hoa.'"

We are headed for Vung Tau, a beach resort on the South China Sea about 125 kilometers east of Ho Chi Minh City. Today, the general has declared a holiday, a day of relaxation after the hectic schedule of the past two and a half weeks. He isn't with us — he's spending the day with his

his daughter and four grandchildren—but he's closed the War Crimes Exhibit and given the whole staff the day off. Aside from Mr. Giai, Miss Phuong, Luu, John, Bruce and I, there's also a young secretary and her boyfriend, another young woman and two young men—all crammed into an old Ford van.

We've made good time so far, cruising along on a four-lane divided highway left behind by the Americans, though now we are traveling on a slower two-lane macadam road. We pass or are passed by other cars periodically, and more frequently a Honda motorbike with Saigon plates overtakes us on its way to the beach, usually with a young man driving and a young woman hanging on behind.

Back in 1967, *Time* magazine did a story about Vung Tau. There was a color photograph of a wide white beach with people on it. I don't remember the other people in that photograph, but I remember vividly a young Vietnamese woman in a tiny bikini. And I remember sitting on the ground in my filthy jungle utilities in the raging heat in the middle of the war, my rifle across my lap and the magazine on top of the rifle, staring at that photograph and trying to comprehend how such a beautiful place and such a beautiful woman could possibly be in Vietnam.

We pass by thatch-roofed houses and flooded fields, ox-carts and peasants in conical hats, stands of rubber trees and clumps of palm trees. The terrain is perfectly flat, so when the coastal mountain range looms up ahead, we can see it for miles. Bare, jagged rock outcroppings dot the mountains, and nothing grows but tough little bushes that look like sagebrush. Deep erosion scars carve vertical gulleys into the slopes. It reminds me of Wyoming or Utah.

"All this used to be heavily forested," says Luu, "but it was all destroyed. Now nothing will grow."

A huge mountain dominates Vung Tau, blocking off one end of the beach and falling sharply into the sea. At its very top stands an enormous white crucifix, gazing out to sea. John says it was built by Diem, and I marvel that it wasn't pulled down at the end of the war. At the base of the mountain lies the rotted, rusting hulk of an oil tanker damaged and beached during the war. John thinks he recalls that it had been owned by Aristotle Onassis, the Greek shipping magnate who married Jackie Kennedy. Beyond the ghostly tanker are the ruins of a hotel where John and his wife had once stayed a decade and a half earlier. Offshore, reachable by walking at low tide, is a small jagged island with several Buddhist shrines and two old Japanese gun emplacements.

The beach itself is magnificent: a wide, clean crescent of sand stretching north at least eight or ten miles to where another spur of the mountain range comes down to the sea. The south end, where we are, is crowded with bathers. Kids are playing soccer on the wet sand or building sand castles, while other kids and adults splash in the surf or ride innertubes and inflatable rafts. People have brought picnic lunches with them, and sit beneath beach umbrellas drinking beer and eating bananas and rice.

After all these years of anticipation, however, there are no bikini-clad women. Bathing suits of both men and women are modest—the women's suits all one-piece—and invariably several sizes too large, and I wonder if the new regime has ruled the woman in the photograph I remember so well to be a symbol of the decadent West. Still, the water is comfortably refreshing and the waves are breaking well enough to get in some good body-surfing.

The only other Westerners besides the three of us are a group of about a dozen Russians—men and women all lined up in folding beach chairs. They are drinking vodka, they are all overweight, and most of them are as red as lobsters. Again, we play our little game of eye-contact, hoping to strike up a conversation—or at least to get some confirmation of our own existence—but the Russians aren't buying it. We might as well be invisible.

In the afternoon, we drive into town for lunch. The proprietor of the restaurant—an older woman with a plump build and a brash good-natured laugh—seems to know Mr. Giai, and she is expecting us. As we drink beer with ice, Mr. Giai tells us that she has operated this restaurant since the time of the French. As he talks, the lights go out and the ceiling fans quietly glide to a halt, but he doesn't seem to notice. When the woman brings our meal—boiled crabs cut into quarters and dried venison cooked in a tangy sauce—he tells her that John, Bruce and I are poets. She thinks that's fantastic, and orders another round of beer for us.

"I wrote a poem once," says Mr. Giai, "a long time ago, when I was a young man. It was just before a big battle with the French." We persuade him to recite it for us while Luu offers an impromptu translation:

> On the eve of the battle,
> my comrades and I find an abandoned cafe by the river.
> We go inside and sit at a table.
> Quat pretends to roll a cigarette.
> Tho orders a beer.

I ask for tea with sugar.
No one knows which of us will be alive tomorrow.

Mr. Giai beams as we applaud. "Thank you," he says, nodding awkwardly, "Thank you. I tried to have the poem published in the army
newspaper, but they told me it was too sentimental."

After lunch, we drive through town and out along the coast road.
The little harbor at Vung Tau is filled with fishing boats, each with a pair
of eyes painted on the prow. Other boats are gliding home from the sea
in ones and twos, the sea sparkling wildly in the late afternoon sun.
Above the harbor, we get out of the van and walk up a steep flight of stairs
to the Pagoda of the Sleeping Buddha, perched on the hillside high
above the sea.

The buddha itself, reclining peacefully on its right side, is a massive
figure easily 30 feet long and polished to a fine amber sheen. An old
monk offers me three sticks of incense. Years before, I had written a poem
called "Souvenirs":

> "Bring me back a souvenir," the captain called.
> "Sure think," I shouted back above the amtrac's roar.

> Later that day,
> the column halted,
> we found a Buddhist temple by the trail.
> Combing through a nearby wood,
> we found a heavy log as well.

> It must have taken more than half an hour,
> but at last we battered in
> the concrete walls so badly
> that the roof collapsed.

> Before it did,
> I took two painted vases
> Buddhists use for burning incense.

> One vase I kept,
> and one I offered proudly to the captain.

I take the incense sticks and hold them while the old man lights
them. Standing before the buddha with the burning sticks pressed between my palms, I bow three times, then place the incense in a large

painted vase. The old monk seems pleased that I know the ritual. As I turn to go, he begins to hammer on a large bronze bell with a wooden mallet. He is waking up the spirits to receive my prayers.

On the way back to Ho Chi Minh City, we are flagged down by a policeman standing in front of a small wooden shack that is clearly some kind of checkpoint. Luu fishes around in his shoulderbag and comes up with some papers which he hands to Mr. Giai, and the two men get out and go over to the shack. In a few minutes, they return and we are on our way again.

"What was that all about?" I ask Luu.

"Just routine," he replies, shrugging his shoulders.

"What were they checking for?"

"Nothing. It's just routine. They stop everyone."

"Do Vietnamese need papers to travel?" I ask.

"From Saigon to Vung Tau?" he asks in return.

"Yes."

"No," he says, but he seems uncomfortable with my questions. I let the matter drop, and soon drift off to sleep.

Back at the hotel, we encounter Linda and one of her colleagues in the lobby. They are just going for a drink at the old Caravelle Hotel — now called the Doc Lap, or Independence — and ask us to join them, which Bruce and I do. The bar on the seventh floor of the Doc Lap is fitted out in what appears to be early 1960s Howard Johnson's furniture, and the decorations are a kind of post-modernist cubist psychedelic. Reggae music blares from a tape-player behind the bar. We order several rounds of "Saigon cocktails," the main ingredient of which seems to be bland orange juice.

Bruce has trouble locating the men's room, but is helped out by several Westerners sitting at a nearby table. When he comes back, he seems mildly amazed by the assistance he has gotten. "They sounded like Russians," he says. All three of them — two men and a woman — are looking at us and smiling. We motion them over to join us.

"You're not Russian, are you?" I ask.

No, they reply, laughing, they are Czechoslovakians, members of an agricultural delegation.

"Why do you think we are Russian?" the woman asks in heavily accented English.

"I didn't think you were Russian," I reply. "That's why I asked. None of the Russians around here will even give us the time of day."

The woman laughs again. "Don't take it too hard," she says, "They won't talk to us, either. They never talk to anybody."

It is getting late. I excuse myself and walk up the street to the square. Tuan, Sanh and Huong are all there, sitting together on a bench. They all smile and wave when they see me. I buy them each a popsicle. Then I tell them that tomorrow I am leaving. "I miss my wife very much," I say, taking her picture from my pocket and showing it to them, "It is time for me to go home."

"This your wife?" Sanh asks.

"Yes."

"She very pretty."

Huong takes the picture in one hand and lightly touches it with the fingers of her other hand, gazing at it for a long time. Then she touches my chest with the palm of her hand, as if patting my heart, and breaks into a smile, the dimple exploding on her cheek. She studies the photograph again. The smile passes and her face darkens. She hands me the picture. "Goodbye," she says in English. It is the first English I have heard her speak.

"You cry again," Sanh says to me, "Why you sad?"

"I'll miss you," I say, "Take care of each other." I stand up and shake hands with Sanh. Then I shake hands with Tuan, who takes my hand firmly and gives me a big smile. Huong will not shake my hand. She looks down at her feet and says something in Vietnamese. Then she looks at me and smiles shyly.

"She wants you to give her a kiss," says Sanh.

Goodbye to All That

From the restaurant of the Cuu Long Hotel, five floors up, the flat green expanse of rice fields on the far side of the Saigon River is still shrouded in morning mist. Dozens of small boats criss-cross the river below me: ferries and fishing boats, tugboats and barges. Off to my right, a deepwater ship is maneuvering out into the current, perhaps leaving the very dock where Graham Greene once watched United States military airplanes off-loaded fully 33 years ago, in the last days of the French Indochina War. The street below is awash with pedestrians, bicycles, motorscooters and Lambrettas, and across Dong Khoi Street, construction workers two floors below me are already busy inside the concrete skeleton of a new building.

Perhaps in another generation or two, no one here will even remember the Majestic Hotel or Tu Do Street or "the ugly statue of the crouching marines." In a history stretching back to Bronze Age drummers on the hills overlooking the Red River Valley, the French — and even the Americans — are just another chapter. Already a new chapter is being written.

Down in the hotel lobby, General Chi, Mr. Giai and Luu are waiting to take us to the airport. The general has brought his six-year-old grandson with him — the oldest of four children by his daughter who lives in Ho Chi Minh City. The boy is dressed in light blue shorts and a matching short-sleeved jacket, and greets us with a shy "hello" in English as the general, like any doting grandparent, beams with pride.

At the airport, we are taken to the head of the ticket line and issued our boarding passes with a minimum of delay. Uniformed customs officers are diligently dismantling the baggage of travelers ahead of us, but a few words from the general are all it takes to get us waved through with not even so much as a cursory inspection. Another uniformed officer reclaims our visas. Our passports have never been stamped, so that now

176

we have no official documentation that we had ever set foot in Vietnam.

There is no way to change my remaining Vietnamese currency back into dollars, so I try to give it to Luu, but he refuses it. "It would not be appropriate," he says, shaking my hand firmly, "Take care of yourself. Thank you for coming. I hope we will meet again."

Mr. Giai gives me a hug. He is so short that I have to bend down to him, so thin and frail that I almost fear I will crush him. "Friends," he says in English. As he turns away, he appears to be wiping tears from his eyes.

The general wants to wait with us, but the officers indicate that he is not allowed in the departure area—another small reminder of the limits of privilege—so we must say goodbye here. It isn't easy. He is a communist general, a former enemy, a man whose political philosophy does not sit well with me. But in the past 16 days, he has been a kind host and solicitous companion, full of humor and grace, and I have grown genuinely fond of him. Perhaps a day will come when I will not have to feel the need to justify my affection for this man who was once my adversary. I extend my hand, but the general brushes it aside and embraces me with both arms, giving me a kiss on each cheek. And then he turns away and is gone.

Most of our fellow passengers waiting in the departure area are Vietnamese—Orderly Departure Program emigrants bound for new lives in the United States or France or Australia. All wear name tags with numbers. Most wear Western-style clothing, and many of the women are wearing make-up. Two teenage girls in blue jeans and lipstick listen to rock-and roll music on a tapeplayer. An old woman weeps inconsolably while younger members of her family look on helplessly. Over in one corner of the room, two United States immigration officials conduct last-minute interviews. The room is strewn with bags and bundles and packages.

A middleaged woman across from us asks in halting English if we will converse with her teenaged son. She tells us she wants him to practice his English, explaining that they will not be permitted to leave the holding camp in the Philippines until his English is deemed adequate. We ask him things like how old is he, what has he studied in school, and what would he like to become. He replies with one- and two-word answers, seemingly unable to look us in the eye or string together more than three words of English in succession.

What are these people leaving behind, I wonder, where are they going and what will their lives be like? Fully one-third of the people living in the American colonies in the 1770s supported the British Crown to the bitter end. They were tarred and feathered, their homes and crops were burned, their businesses confiscated by the victorious "patriots." Some were lynched, others beaten by mobs. In the aftermath of Yorktown, often with nothing but the clothes on their backs, they fled for their lives or were physically driven out, emigrating to Nova Scotia, Newfoundland, Bermuda and the Bahamas.

In 1982, Anne and I spent a week on Elbow Cay off Abaco in the Bahamas. We did our shopping in a small grocery store in the little community of Hope Town. In the course of a casual conversation one day, the store owner told us that his ancestors had come to Hope Town from South Carolina in 1782. "We get by here all right," he had said, "but it's nothing like we had in the Carolinas. Those rebel bastards stole our country from us, don't you know? That's all they were, really—just traitors."

There are always winners and losers.

Home

True to his word, John McAuliff got us out of Bangkok on schedule, but a snowstorm in Korea delayed us by seven hours, causing me to miss my connecting flight out of New York's Kennedy International. We arrived at Kennedy at 2 a.m., Saturday morning, January 4, 1986, and rather than wait until 8 a.m. for the next available flight, I rented a car and drove the last 100 miles home, arriving at 5:30 a.m. It cost me nearly a dollar a mile, but it was worth it.

Anne had bought and decorated a small Christmas tree, and the lights were winking in the predawn darkness as I walked in to find her asleep on the couch. She had decorated the vestibule with all the Christmas cards we'd received in my absence, and around the base of the tree were all of our presents, still unopened. Together we opened the presents, then spent the rest of the day in bed, alternately sleeping and getting to know each other again. It was the happiest "Christmas Day" I've ever spent, even if it was a little late.

Two days later, I found out that even as we were being told by our Vietnamese hosts that travel to central Vietnam was not possible, eight other American veterans on another trip were walking the streets of Hue, chipping spent M-16 rounds from the walls of the Citadel and recalling old and bitter battles. What had gone wrong? Why had I been denied the opportunity to do likewise? Was it proof-positive of wily communist perfidy, or merely some bureaucratic bungle my hosts were too embarrassed to acknowledge — or something else I haven't even thought of?

My guess is that by the time General Chi realized we wanted to go to central Vietnam, it was too late to make the arrangements. There *had* been a severe typhoon just before we arrived, perhaps offering the general a convenient excuse to avoid having to acknowledge to us that the creaking bureaucracy and limited resources of the Vietnamese could not accommodate so radical a change in the planned agenda. Not under-

179

standing the nature of communications in the United States, he didn't anticipate how easily I would be able to learn that other Americans had been where we had wanted to go. I'm just guessing. I doubt that I will ever know for sure.

But I do know now that it doesn't really matter. My initial disappointment has long since given way to the realization that I did indeed see and do what I went to Vietnam to see and do. Now when I think of Vietnam, I will not see in my mind's eye the barbed wire and the grim patrols and the violent death that always exploded with no warning. Now I will see those graceful fishing boats gliding out of the late afternoon sun across the South China Sea toward safe harbor at Vung Tau, and the buffalo boys riding the backs of those great gray beasts in the fields along the road to Tay Ninh. Now I will not hear the guns, but rather the gentle rhythmic beat of rice stalks striking the threshing mats.

I do not think for a moment that all is well in Vietnam. I had not expected to find a socialist workers' paradise, and the effects of eighty years of colonial exploitation, thirty years of war, and ten years of economic and diplomatic isolation were everywhere painfully evident, as was the austere presence of a government I can hardly feel too comfortable about. Along with my memories of Mr. Hung and Miss Bich and Mr. Giai, I will carry forever the kiss I received from Nguyen Thi My Huong.

But the Vietnamese have no corner on the market for hardship, and the world is full of governments I can't begin to approve of—many of them among the staunchest allies and clients of the United States of America. At least in Vietnam today, no one is dropping bombs or burning villages or defoliating forests, and what is taking place is not being done in my name or with my tax dollars, and no one is asking me to participate. It is their country, finally, and it is their business what they do with it. The Vietnamese have burdens of their own to bear; they have no need and no use for my anguish or my guilt. My war is over. It ended long ago.

Epilogue

More than 20 years ago, the president of the United States told us that if we did not stop the communists in Vietnam, we would have to fight them on the sands of Waikiki. Things didn't work out the way we expected them to, but the hotels along the beach in Honolulu seem to be doing just fine, nevertheless. Now we are being told that if we don't stop the communists in Nicaragua, we will have to fight them in the streets of Brownsville, Texas.

As far back as 1935, two-time Congressional Medal of Honor winner Major General Smedley Butler offered this warning to the American people: "We must give up carrying on offensive warfare and imposing our wills upon other people in distant places. Such doctrine is un–American and vicious." No one paid much attention back then to this hero who characterized his 33-year Marine Corps career as that of "a racketeer for capitalism, a high-priced muscle man for Big Business, for Wall Street and for the bankers." But one might have hoped that the American experience in Vietnam would finally have driven his message home.

Sadly, that has thus far not been the case. Since the end of the Vietnam war, the United States has dispatched the Marines to Lebanon at a cost of nearly 300 American lives, invaded the tiny Caribbean island of Grenada with its army smaller than the police department of Providence, Rhode Island, sent military advisors to El Salvador, established what amounts to a permanent military presence in Honduras, baited and bombed Libya, pressed for the militarization of Costa Rica — the only stable democracy in Central America — and pursued a single-mindedly obsessive policy of intervention in Nicaragua with the open goal of toppling a widely popular revolutionary government that freed Nicaraguans from the squalor and oppression of more than forty years of U.S.-backed dictatorial rule by the hated Somoza family.

True, the Soviet Union and many other countries have also been up to no good, and with distressing frequency. But I am neither Russian nor South African nor anything other than an American. As Bruce Springsteen would say, "I was born in the U.S.A." I love my country, and I find it infinitely sad that so often the best defense we can offer for ourselves is that "the Russians are doing it, too."

And now, as I write this, we are faced with the prospect of war in Nicaragua, a war that in many ways is already upon us. I am not convinced that we have anything to fear from an impoverished agrarian nation with a total population less than that of the city of Philadelphia. But I believe we have much to fear from a government that tries to persuade us that we do.

Or will it be Libya? Or the Philippines? Or who knows where? Unless we can begin to learn from the American experience in Vietnam, unless we can begin to study our own history rather than repeating endlessly the tenets of our national mythology, it is only a question of time before our children become the next generation of "Vietnam veterans." Our leaders will tell our children it is their patriotic duty to defend their country. Straight-faced, full of piety and righteousness, they will tell us that they have no choice except to fight. And then they will send our children off to wage war against the children of another Nguyen Thi Na. Old Mrs. Na, who wanted little else than for us to stop killing her children and go home.

Afterword

I wish to make it clear that the recollections, reflections and opinions expressed in this book are mine alone. The trip itself was a shared experience, but I cannot and do not attempt to speak for my two traveling companions, John Balaban and Bruce Weigl, and they ought not to be held accountable for anything contained herein—except for their two fine poems, which they have graciously permitted me to include.

Thanks to the following people, who in various ways helped to make my trip possible, or assisted in the preparation of this book and the articles which preceded it: John McAuliff, Bill Quesenbery, Charles Layton, Nguyen Dang Quang, Tran Trong Khanh, Nguyen Thanh Chau, Tran Kinh Chi and his staff, Robbie Franklin, Horace Coleman, Jenny Beer, Ben & Janet Kalkstein, David & Suzy Kalkstein, Warren & Pat Witte, Ed & Gloria Finkle, Bob & Joann Evans, Steve Gulick & Glenavie Norton, the Rev. John & Evelyn Ehrhart, and of course, my wife, Anne Gulick Ehrhart.

W.D. Ehrhart
Philadelphia
August 9, 1986

Military History of W.D. Ehrhart

W.D. Ehrhart formally enlisted in the Marines on 11 April 1966, while still in high school, beginning active duty on 17 June. He graduated from basic recruit training at the Marine Corps Recruit Depot, Parris Island, South Carolina, as a private first class on 12 August and completed his basic infantry training at Camp Lejeune, North Carolina, on 12 September 1966. (While at Parris Island, he qualified as a rifle sharpshooter on 18 July 1966, subsequently qualifying as a rifle expert on 11 April 1968 and as a pistol sharpshooter on 24 April 1969.)

Assigned to the field of combat intelligence, Ehrhart spent 10 October to 15 December 1966 with Marine Air Group 26, a helicopter unit based at New River Marine Corps Air Facility, North Carolina, meanwhile completing a clerk typist course at Camp Lejeune in November 1966 and graduating first in his class from the Enlisted Basic Amphibious Intelligence School at Little Creek Amphibious Base, Norfolk, Va., in December 1966. He also completed a Marine Corps Institute combat intelligence correspondence course in December while at New River.

Before leaving for Vietnam on 9 February 1967, Ehrhart received additional combat training with the 3rd Replacement Company, Staging Battalion, Camp Pendleton, California, in January and February. Upon arrival in Vietnam, he was assigned to the 1st Battalion, 1st Marine Regiment, first as an intelligence assistant, later as assistant intelligence chief. In March 1967, he was temporarily assigned to the Sukiran Army Education Center, Okinawa, where he graduated first in his class from a course in basic Vietnamese terminology before returning to permanent assignment.

While in Vietnam, Ehrhart participated in the following combat operations: Stone, Lafayette, Early, Canyon, Calhoun, Pike, Medina, Lancaster, Kentucky I, Kentucky II, Kentucky III, Con Thien, Newton,

Osceola II, and Hue City. He was promoted to lance corporal on 1 April 1967 and to corporal on 1 July 1967.

Ehrhart was awarded the Purple Heart for wounds received during Operation Hue City, a commendation from the commanding general of the 1st Marine Division, two Presidential Unit Citations, the Navy Combat Action Ribbon, the Vietnam Service Medal with three stars, and the Vietnamese Campaign Medal. He completed his Vietnam tour on 28 February 1968.

Ehrhart was next assigned to the 2nd Marine Air Wing Headquarters Group at Cherry Point Marine Corps Air Station, North Carolina, from 30 March to 10 June 1968, where he was promoted to sergeant on 1 April. After a brief assignment with the Headquarters Squadron of Marine Air Group 15 based at Iwakuni Marine Corps Air Station, Japan, he was then reassigned to Marine Aerial Refueler Transport Squadron 152, Futema Marine Corps Air Facility, Okinawa, from 20 July to 30 October 1968, where he received a commanding officer's meritorious mast.

Ehrhart completed his active duty with Marine Fighter Attack Squadron 122, based alternately at Iwakuni and Cubi Point Naval Air Station, Philippines, from 31 October 1968 to 30 May 1969. While in the Philippines, he completed a field course on jungle environmental survival in February 1969.

On 10 June 1969, Ehrhart was separated from active duty, receiving the Good Conduct Medal. While on inactive reserve, he was promoted to staff sergeant on 1 July 1971. He received an honorable discharge on 10 April 1972.

Index

In Vietnamese, the first word of a person's name is the equivalent of a Western last name, and all entries in this index are alphabetized accordingly. For example, General Tran Kinh Chi is indexed under Tran Kinh Chi, General. "Tran" is in effect a *clan* name, however, which one does not arrogate to oneself; therefore, "General Chi" is the normal form of address.

Numbers in **boldface** indicate photographs.

About the Author

W.D. Ehrhart was born in 1948 and grew up in Perkasie, Pennsylvania. He holds a bachelor's degree from Swarthmore College and a master's from the University of Illinois at Chicago. He has worked variously as a merchant seaman, forklift operator and warehouseman, roofer, legal aide, newspaper reporter, editor, and teacher at both the high school and college levels. He lives in Philadelphia, with his wife, Anne, and daughter, Leela, and teaches English literature at Germantown Friends School.

After his service in the Marines, Ehrhart became active in Vietnam Veterans Against the War, contributing poetry to the 1972 VVAW-sponsored anthology, *Winning Hearts and Minds*. In 1975, he and fellow Vietnam veteran Jan Barry founded East River Anthology, publishers of *Demilitarized Zones* and *Peace Is Our Profession*. Since then, his prose and poetry have appeared in several dozen anthologies and several hundred periodicals including *New Letters, The Virginia Quarterly Review, TriQuarterly*, and *The Chronicle of Higher Education*.